The Curious Incident of the Dog in the Night-Time

Mark Haddon is the author of *The Red House*, *A Spot of Bother* and *The Curious Incident of the Dog in the Night-Time*. He has also published a collection of poetry, *The Talking Horse and the Sad Girl and the Village Under the Sea*. His work for television and radio includes *Coming Down the Mountain* and *Microsoap*. *Polar Bears* (2010) was Mark Haddon's first work for the theatre.

Simon Stephens began his theatrical career as a tutor in the Young Writers' Programme at the Royal Court Theatre, London. His plays for theatre include *Bluebird* (Royal Court Theatre Upstairs, 1998, directed by Gordon Anderson); *Herons* (Royal Court Theatre Upstairs, 2001); *Port* (Royal Exchange Theatre, Manchester, 2002); *One Minute* (Crucible Theatre, Sheffield, 2003 and Bush Theatre, London, 2004); *Christmas* (Bush Theatre, 2004); *Country Music* (Royal Court Theatre Upstairs, 2004); *On the Shore of the Wide World* (Royal Exchange Theatre and National Theatre, London, 2005); *Motortown* (Royal Court Theatre Downstairs, 2006); *Pornography* (Deutsches Schauspielhaus, Hanover, 2007; Edinburgh Festival/Birmingham Rep, 2008 and Tricycle Theatre, London, 2009); *Harper Regan* (National Theatre, 2008); *Sea Wall* (Bush Theatre, 2008/Traverse Theatre, Edinburgh, 2009); *Heaven* (Traverse Theatre, 2009); *Punk Rock* (Lyric Hammersmith, London and Royal Exchange Theatre, 2009); *The Trial of Ubu* (Essen Schauspielhaus/Toneelgroep Amsterdam, 2010 and Hampstead Theatre, London, 2012); *A Thousand Stars Explode in the Sky* (co-written with David Eldridge and Robert Holman; Lyric Hammersmith, 2010); *Marine Parade* (co-written with Mark Eitzel; Brighton International Festival, 2010); *T5* (Traverse Theatre, 2010); and *Wastwater* (Royal Court Theatre Downstairs, 2011); *Three Kingdoms* (Lyric Hammersmith, 2012). His radio plays include *Five Letters Home to Elizabeth* (BBC Radio 4, 2001) and *Digging* (BBC Radio 4, 2003). His screenwriting includes the two-part serial *Dive* (with Dominic Savage) for Granada/BBC (2009) and a short film adaptation of *Pornography* for Channel 4's 'Coming Up' series (2009). Awards include the Pearson Award for Best New Play, 2001, for *Port*; Olivier Award for Best New Play for *On the Shore of the Wide World*, 2005; and *Theater Heute*'s Best Foreign Play for *Motortown* (2007), *Pornography* (2008) and *Wastwater* (2011).

Simon Stephens

The Curious Incident of the Dog in the Night-Time

Adapted from the novel by Mark Haddon

methuen | drama

LONDON · NEW YORK · OXFORD · NEW DELHI · SYDNEY

METHUEN DRAMA
Bloomsbury Publishing Plc
50 Bedford Square, London, WC1B 3DP, UK
1385 Broadway, New York, NY 10018, USA
29 Earlsfort Terrace, Dublin 2, Ireland

BLOOMSBURY, METHUEN DRAMA and the Methuen Drama logo
are trademarks of Bloomsbury Publishing Plc

The Curious Incident of the Dog in the Night-Time by Mark Haddon

Adapted for the stage by Simon Stephens

The Curious Incident of the Dog in the Night-Time
was first published in 2003 by Jonathan Cape

This stage adaptation first published in Great Britain 2012 by Methuen Drama
Reprinted with changes in 2013 by Bloomsbury Methuen Drama
Reprinted 2013 (three times), 2014 (four times) and 2015 (five times),
2016 (twice), 2017, 2018, 2019 (twice), 2020, 2021

A catalogue record for this book is available from the British Library.

A catalog record for this book is available from the Library of Congress.

ISBN: PB: 978-1-4081-7335-0
ePDF: 978-1-4081-7337-4
ePUB: 978-1-4081-7336-7

Series: Modern Plays

Typeset by Mark Heslington Ltd, Scarborough, North Yorkshire
Printed and bound in Great Britain

To find out more about our authors and books visit
www.bloomsbury.com and sign up for our newsletters.

National Theatre

Founded in 1963, and established on London's South Bank in 1976, the National Theatre is dedicated to the constant revitalisation of the great traditions of the British stage and to expanding the horizons of audiences and artists alike. In its three theatres, it presents an eclectic mix of new plays and classics from the world repertoire with seven or eight productions in repertory at any one time. The National Theatre aspires to reflect in its repertoire the diversity of the nation's culture.

The National takes a particular responsibility for the creation of new work – using the NT Studio as a space for research and development for the NT's stages and the theatre as a whole. Through its Learning programme, it invites people of all ages to discover the NT's repertoire, the skills and excitement of theatre-making, and the building itself.

With a commitment to openness, wide-reaching engagement and access for everyone, the National shares its resources, energy and creativity with audiences and theatre-makers around the globe, offering an extensive programme of public engagement activities, touring and broadcasting in the UK and internationally, and creating innovative digital content.

Between 20 and 26 new productions are staged each year in one of the NT's three theatres. In 2011–12, the National's total reach was 3.2 million people worldwide, through attendances on the South Bank, in the West End, on tour, and through National Theatre Live, the digital broadcast of live performances to cinema screens all over the world.

Chairman of the NT Board **John Makinson**
Director of the National Theatre **Nicholas Hytner**
Executive Director **Nick Starr**
Chief Operating Officer **Lisa Burger**
Deputy Executive Director **Kate Horton**
Associate Producer **Pádraig Cusack**

Information: +44(0)20 7452 3400
Box office: +44(0)20 7452 3000
National Theatre, South Bank, London SE1 9PX
nationaltheatre.org.uk
Registered Charity No: 224223

Cast list for the original production, opening in the National
Theatre's Cottesloe Theatre, 2 August 2012:

Christopher Boone	**Luke Treadaway***
Siobhan	**Niamh Cusack**
Ed	**Paul Ritter**
Judy	**Nicola Walker**
Mrs Alexander	**Una Stubbs**
Mrs Shears	**Sophie Duval**
Mr Thompson	**Matthew Barker**
No. 40	**Rhiannon Harper-Rafferty**
Roger Shears	**Nick Sidi**
Reverend Peters	**Howard Ward**

All other parts played by members of the Company

For the transfer to the Apollo Theatre, Shaftesbury Avenue, from 1
March 2013:

Seán Gleeson took over from Paul Ritter, **Holly Aird** from Nicola
Walker, and **Tilly Tremayne** from Una Stubbs; **Johnny Gibbon**
played Christopher at some performances, and **Jake Ferretti**,
Jane Lambert, **David Mara** and **Claire Winsper** also joined the
ensemble.

Director	**Marianne Elliott**
Designer	**Bunny Christie**
Lighting Designer	**Paule Constable**
Video Designer	**Finn Ross**
Movement Directors	**Scott Graham and Steven Hoggett** for Frantic Assembly
Music	**Adrian Sutton**
Sound Designer	**Ian Dickinson** for Autograph
Associate Director	**Nadia Fall**
Fight Director	**Kate Waters**
Resident Director	**Katy Rudd**

Characters

Christopher Boone
Siobhan
Ed
Judy
Mrs Alexander / Posh Woman / Voice Six
Mrs Shears / Mrs Gascoyne / Voice One / Woman on Train /
Woman on Heath / Shopkeeper
Roger (Mr Shears) / Duty Sergeant / Voice Two / Mr Wise /
Man behind Counter / Drunk One
Policeman One / Mr Thompson / Voice Three / Drunk Two /
Man with Socks / Man on Phone / London Transport
Policeman / London Policeman
Number 40 / Voice Five / Lady in Street / Information /
Punk Girl
Reverend Peters / Rhodri / Uncle Terry / Voice Four /
Station Policeman / Station Guard

All actors remain on stage unless prescribed otherwise.

There is also a dead dog. With a fork sticking out of it.

*Scenes run into one another without interruption regardless of
alterations in space or time or chronology.*

Part One

A dead dog lies in the middle of the stage. A large garden fork is sticking out of its side.

Christopher Boone, *15 years old, stands on one side of it. His 42-year-old neighbour* **Mrs Shears** *stands on the other.*

They stand for a while without saying anything. The rest of the company watch, waiting to see who is going to dare to speak first.

Mrs Shears   What in fuck's name have you done to my dog?

Christopher *is frozen to the spot.*

Mrs Shears   Oh no. Oh no. Oh no. Oh my fucking Christ.

Christopher's *teacher, 27-year-old* **Siobhan**, *opens* **Christopher**'s *book. She reads from it.*

Siobhan   It was seven minutes after midnight. The dog was lying on the grass in the middle of the lawn in front of Mrs Shears' house.

Mrs Shears   Get away from my dog.

Siobhan   Its eyes were closed. It looked as if it was running on its side, the way dogs run when they think they are chasing a cat in a dream. But the dog was not running or asleep. The dog was dead.

Mrs Shears   Get away from my dog.

Siobhan   There was a garden fork sticking out of the dog. The dog was called Wellington. It belonged to Mrs Shears who was our friend. She lived on the opposite side of the road, two houses to the left.

Mrs Shears   Get away from my dog.

Christopher *takes two steps away from the dog.*

Siobhan   My name is Christopher John Francis Boone. I know all the countries of the world and the capital cities. And every prime number up to 7507.

Mrs Shears   Get away from my dog for Christ's sake.

Christopher *puts his hands over his ears. He closes his eyes. He rolls forward. He presses his forehead onto the grass. He starts groaning.*

Siobhan   After twelve and a half minutes a policeman arrived. He had a big orange leaf stuck to the bottom of his shoe which was poking out from one side. This is good Christopher. It's quite exciting. I like the details. They make it more realistic.

Policeman One *enters. He has a big orange leaf stuck to the bottom of his shoe, which is poking out from one side. He squats next to* **Christopher**.

Siobhan   He squatted down next to me. He said to me:

Christopher *stops groaning.*

Policeman One   Would you like to tell me what's going on here, young man?

Christopher *lifts his head from the ground.*

There is some time.

Christopher *looks at the policeman.*

There is some time.

Siobhan   I do not tell lies. Mother used to say that this was because I was a good person. But it is not because I am a good person. It is because I can't tell lies.

Christopher   The dog is dead.

Policeman One   I'd got that far.

Christopher   I think someone killed the dog.

Policeman One   How old are you?

Christopher I'm fifteen years and three months and two days.

Policeman One And what precisely are you doing in the garden?

Christopher I'm talking to you.

Policeman One OK, what were you doing in the garden in the first place?

Christopher I was holding the dog.

Policeman One Why were you holding the dog? Why were you holding the dog?

Christopher I like dogs.

Policeman One Did you kill the dog?

Christopher I did not kill the dog.

Policeman One Is this your fork?

Christopher No.

Policeman One You seem very upset about this.

I'm going to ask you once again.

Christopher *starts groaning.*

Policeman One Terrific.

Christopher *carries on groaning.*

Policeman One Young man I'm going to ask you to stop making that noise and to stand up please calmly and quietly.

Christopher *carries on groaning.*

Policeman One Marvellous. Great. Just flipping –

Policeman One *tries to lift him up by his arm.*

Christopher *screams. He hits* **Policeman One**, *who stares at* **Christopher**. *For a while the two look at one another, neither entirely sure what to say or quite believing what has just happened.*

Policeman One   I'm arresting you for assaulting a police officer.

I strongly advise you to get into the back of the police car because if you try any of that monkey business again you little shit I am going to seriously lose my rag. Is that understood?

Siobhan   I find people confusing. This is for two main reasons. The first main reason is that people do a lot of talking without using any words. Siobhan says that if you raise one eyebrow it can mean lots of different things. It can mean, 'I want to do sex with you.' I never said that.

Christopher   Yes you did.

Siobhan   I didn't use those words Christopher.

Christopher   You did on 12 September last year. At first break.

Siobhan   And it can also mean, 'I think that what you just said was very stupid.'

Duty Sergeant   Could you take your laces out of your shoes please Christopher?

Christopher *does*.

Duty Sergeant   Thank you. Could you empty your pocket onto the desk please?

Christopher   Is that in case I have anything in them that I could use to kill myself or escape or attack a policeman with?

The **Duty Sergeant** *looks at him for a beat*.

Duty Sergeant   That's right.

Christopher   I've got a Swiss Army knife but I only use that for doing 'odd jobs' not for stabbing things or hurting people.

Duty Sergeant   Jolly good.

Christopher *empties his pockets.*

Voice Four   A piece of string.

Voice Five   A piece of a wooden puzzle.

Voice Six   Three pellets of rat food for Toby, my pet rat.

Voice Four   £1.47 (this was made up of a £1 coin, a 20p coin, two 10p coins, a 5p coin and a 2p coin).

Voice Six   A red paperclip.

Voice Four   A key for the front door.

Voice Five   A Swiss Army knife with thirteen attachments including a wire stripper and a saw and a toothpick and tweezers.

Duty Sergeant   Could you take your watch off please Christopher?

Christopher   No.

Duty Sergeant   I'm sorry Christopher?

Christopher   I need my watch to know exactly what time it is.

Duty Sergeant   Take your watch off, please Christopher. Christopher please will you take your watch off. I'm asking you for a final time.

Give it here lad.

The **Duty Sergeant** *tries to take the watch.*

Christopher *starts screaming.*

The **Duty Sergeant** *stops. He moves away. He nods his head.*
Christopher *stops screaming.*

Duty Sergeant   It's all right son. You keep it.

Christopher *calms down.*

Duty Sergeant   Do you have any family Christopher?

Christopher   Yes I do.

Duty Sergeant   And who is your family?

Christopher   Father and Mother but Mother's dead. And also Uncle Terry who is in Sunderland. He is my father's brother and my grandparents too but three of them are dead and Grandma Burton is in a home because she has senile dementia and thinks I'm someone on television.

Duty Sergeant   Right. Lovely. Do you know your father's phone number Christopher?

Christopher *turns to* **Ed**. **Ed** *looks at him. He holds his hand out in front of him with his fingers stretched.* **Christopher** *does the same. They touch fingers. Then let go.*

Christopher   I could see the Milky Way as we drove towards the town centre.

Ed   Could you?

Christopher   Some people think the Milky Way is a long line of stars, but it isn't. Our galaxy is a huge disc of stars of millions of light years across and the solar system is somewhere near the outer edge of the disc.

Ed   Is that right?

Christopher   For a long time scientists were puzzled by the fact that the sky is dark at night even though there are billions of stars in the universe and there must be stars in every direction you look, so that the sky should be full of starlight because there is very little in the way to stop the light reaching earth.

Ed *stares at him. Says nothing.*

Christopher   Then they worked out that the universe was expanding, that the stars were all rushing away from one another after the Big Bang and the further the stars were away from us the faster they were moving, some of them nearly as fast as the speed of light, which was why their light never reached us.

Ed   Terrific.

Duty Sergeant   Christopher. Mr Boone. Could you come this way please?

Christopher   Are you going to interview me and record the interview?

Duty Sergeant   I don't think there will be any need for that.

I've spoken to your father and he says you didn't mean to hit the policeman.

Did you mean to hit the policeman?

Christopher   Yes.

Duty Sergeant   But you didn't mean to hurt the policeman?

Christopher   No. I didn't mean to hurt the policeman I just wanted him to stop touching me.

Duty Sergeant   You know that it's wrong to hit a policeman don't you?

Christopher   I do.

Duty Sergeant   Did you kill the dog Christopher?

Christopher   I didn't kill the dog.

Duty Sergeant   Do you know that it is wrong to lie to a policeman and that you can get into a very great deal of trouble if you do?

Christopher   Yes.

Duty Sergeant   Do you know who killed the dog?

Christopher   No.

Duty Sergeant   Are you telling the truth?

Christopher   Yes. I always tell the truth.

Duty Sergeant   Right. I'm going to give you a caution.

Christopher   Is that going to be on a piece of paper like a certificate I can keep?

Duty Sergeant   No. A caution means that we are going to keep a record of what you did, that you hit a policeman but that it was an accident and that you didn't mean to hurt the policeman.

Christopher   But it wasn't an accident.

Ed   Christopher, please.

Duty Sergeant   If you get into any more trouble we will take out this record and see that you have been given a caution and we will take things much more seriously. Do you understand what I'm saying?

Christopher   Yes.

Siobhan   The second main reason is that people often talk using metaphors. These are examples of metaphors.

Voice One   I am going to seriously lose my rag.

Voice Two   He was the apple of her eye

Voice Three   They had a skeleton in the cupboard.

Voice Four   We had a real pig of a day.

Voice Five   The dog was stone dead.

Siobhan   The word metaphor means carrying something from one place to another and it is when you describe something by using a word for something that it isn't. This means that the word metaphor is a metaphor. Wow. That's clever.

Christopher   It's true.

Siobhan   Yes. I think it should be called a lie because a pig is not like a day and people do not have skeletons in their cupboards. And when I try and make a picture of the phrase in my head it just confuses me because imagining an apple in someone's eye doesn't have anything to do with liking someone a lot and it makes you forget what the person was talking about.

Christopher *turns to* **Ed**.

Christopher   I'm sorry.

Ed   It's OK.

Christopher   I didn't kill Wellington.

Ed   I know.

Christopher you have to stay out of trouble, OK?

Christopher   I didn't know I was going to get into trouble.
I like Wellington and I went to say hello to him, but I didn't
know that someone had killed him.

Ed   Just try and keep your nose out of other people's
business.

Christopher   I am going to find out who killed Wellington.

Ed   Were you listening to what I was saying, Christopher?

Christopher   Yes I was listening to what you were saying
but when someone gets murdered you have to find out who
did it so that they can be punished.

Ed   It's a bloody dog Christopher, a bloody dog.

Christopher   I think dogs are important too. I think some
dogs are cleverer than some people. Steve, for example, who
comes to school on Thursdays needs help eating his food
and he probably couldn't even fetch a stick.

Ed   Leave it.

Christopher   I wonder if the police will find out who killed
him and punish the person.

Ed   I said leave it for God's sake.

Christopher   Are you sad about Wellington?

Ed   Yes Christopher you could say that. You could very well
say that.

Siobhan *reads more from the book.*

Siobhan   Mother died two years ago.

I came home from school one day and no one answered the door, so I went and found the secret key that we keep under a flowerpot outside the kitchen window. I let myself into the house and wiped my feet on the mat. I put the key in the bowl on the table. I took my coat off and hung it by the side of the fridge so it would be ready for school the next day and gave three pellets of rat food to Toby who is my pet rat. I made myself a raspberry milkshake and heated it up in the microwave. Then I went up to my bedroom and turned on my bedroom light and played six games of Tetris and got to level 38 which is my fourth best ever score.

An hour later Father came home from work.

Ed   Christopher have you seen your mum?

Christopher   No.

Siobhan   He went downstairs and started making some phone calls. I did not hear what he said. Then he came up to my room and said he had to go out for a while and he wasn't sure how long he would be. He said that if I needed anything I should call him on his mobile phone.

He was away for two and a half hours. When he came back I went downstairs.

Ed   I'm afraid you won't be seeing your mother for a while.

Christopher   Why not?

Ed   Your mother has had to go into hospital.

Christopher   Can we visit her?

Ed   No.

Christopher   Why can't we?

Ed   She needs rest. She needs to be on her own.

Christopher   Is it a psychiatric hospital?

Ed   No. It's an ordinary hospital. She has a problem . . . a problem with her heart.

Christopher   We will need to take food to her.

Ed   I'll take some to her during the day when you're at school and I'll give it to the doctors and they can give it to your mum, OK?

Christopher   But you can't cook.

Ed   Christopher. Look. I'll buy some ready-made stuff from Marks & Spencer and take those in. She likes those.

Christopher   I'll make her a get-well card.

If I make her a get-well card will you take it in for her tomorrow?

Siobhan   How are you today Christopher?

Christopher   I'm very well thank you.

Siobhan   That's good.

Christopher   In the bus on the way to school we passed four red cars in a row.

Siobhan   Four?

Christopher   So today is a Good Day.

Siobhan   Great. I am glad.

Christopher   I've decided I am going to try and find out who killed Wellington because a Good Day is a day for projects and planning things.

Siobhan   Who's Wellington?

Christopher   Wellington is a dog that used to belong to my neighbour Mrs Shears who is our friend but he is dead now because somebody killed him by putting a garden fork through him. And I found him and then a policeman thought I'd killed him but I hadn't and then he tried to touch me so I hit him and then I had to go to the police station.

Siobhan   Gosh.

Christopher   And I am going to find out who really killed Wellington and make it a project. Even though Father told me not to.

Siobhan   Did he?

Christopher   Yes.

Siobhan   I see.

Christopher   I don't always do what I'm told.

Siobhan   Why?

Christopher   Because when people tell you what to do it is usually confusing and does not make sense. For example people often say 'Be quiet' but they don't tell you how long to be quiet for.

Siobhan   No. Why did your father tell you not to try to find out who killed Wellington, Christopher?

Christopher   I don't know.

Siobhan   Christopher if your father's told you not to do something maybe you shouldn't do it.

Well, we're meant to be writing stories today, so why don't you write about what happened to Wellington?

Christopher   OK I will.

Siobhan   I can help you.

Christopher   Will you help me with the spelling and the grammar and the footnotes?

Ed   Christopher, I'm sorry your mother's died.

She's had a heart attack.

It wasn't expected.

Christopher   What kind of heart attack?

Ed   I don't know what kind of heart attack. Now isn't the moment Christopher to be asking questions like that.

Christopher   It was probably an aneurysm.

Ed   I'm sorry Christopher, I'm really sorry.

Mrs Shears' *house is assembled.*

Siobhan   That evening I went round to Mrs Shears' house and knocked on the door and waited for her to answer it.

Mrs Shears *answers her door. She is drinking a cup of tea.*

Mrs Shears   What are you doing here?

Christopher   I wanted to come and tell you that I didn't kill Wellington. And also I want to find out who killed him.

Mrs Shears   Christopher, I really don't think I want to see you right now.

Christopher   Do you know who killed Wellington?

Mrs Shears   Can you go now Christopher.

Christopher   I wanted to see if the fork was in the shed.

Mrs Shears   If you don't go now I will call the police again.

Christopher   Reverend Peters, where is heaven?

Reverend Peters   I'm sorry Christopher?

Christopher   In our universe whereabouts is it exactly?

Reverend Peters   It's not in our universe. It's another kind of place altogether.

Christopher   There isn't anything outside our universe Reverend Peters. There isn't another kind of place altogether. Except there might be if you go through a black hole. But a black hole is what is called a singularity which means its impossible to find out what is on the other side because the gravity of a black hole is so big that even electromagnetic waves like light can't get out of it, and electromagnetic waves are how we get information about things which are far away. And if heaven is on the other side of a black hole then dead people would have to be fired into space on a rocket to get there and they aren't or people would notice.

Reverend Peters *looks at him for a while before he responds.*

Reverend Peters   Well when I say heaven is outside our universe it's really just a manner of speaking. I suppose what it really means is that they are with God.

Christopher   But where is God?

Reverend Peters   Christopher we should talk about this on another day when I have more time.

Siobhan   The next day was Saturday and there is not much to do on a Saturday unless Father takes me out somewhere on an outing to the boating lake or to the garden centre, but on this Saturday England were playing Romania at football which meant that we weren't going to go on an outing because Father wanted to watch the match on the television. So I made a decision. I decided to do some more detection. I decided to go out on my own.

Mr Thompson   Can I help you?

Christopher   Do you know who killed Wellington?

Mr Thompson   Who are you?

Christopher   I'm Christopher Boone from number 36 and I know you. You're Mr Thompson.

Mr Thompson   I'm Mr Thompson's brother.

Christopher   Do you know who killed Wellington?

Mr Thompson   Who the fuck is Wellington?

Christopher   Mrs Shears' dog. Mrs Shears is from number 41.

Mr Thompson   Someone killed her dog?

Christopher   With a fork.

Mr Thompson   Jesus Christ.

Christopher   A garden fork.

Mr Thompson   Oh.

Christopher   Do you know who killed him?

Mr Thompson   I haven't a bloody clue.

Christopher   Did you see anything suspicious on Thursday evening?

Mr Thompson   Look son, do you really think you should be going round asking questions like this?

Christopher   Yes, because I want to find out who killed Wellington and I am writing a book about it.

Mr Thompson   Well I was in Colchester on Thursday so you're asking the wrong bloke.

Christopher   Thank you.

Number 40   It's Christopher isn't it?

Christopher   Yes it is. Do you know who killed Wellington?

Number 40   No. No. I don't. No. I'm sorry.

Christopher   Did you see anything suspicious on Thursday evening, which might be a clue?

Number 40   Like what?

Christopher   Like strangers or the sound of people arguing.

Number 40   I didn't Christopher, no.

Christopher   Do you know of anyone who might want to make Mrs Shears sad?

Number 40   Perhaps you should be talking to your father about this.

Christopher   I can't talk to my father about it because he told me to stay out of other people's business.

Number 40   Well maybe he has a point Christopher.

Christopher   So you don't know anything that might be a clue.

Number 40   No. You be careful young man.

Christopher   I will be. Thank you for helping me with my questions.

Do you know who killed Wellington on Thursday night?

Mr Wise   Bloody hell. Policemen really are getting younger aren't they?

Mr Wise *laughs*. **Christopher** *walks away*.

Christopher   Do you know anything about Wellington getting killed?

Mrs Alexander   I'm afraid you're going to have to say that again. I'm a little deaf.

Christopher   Do you know anything about Wellington getting killed?

Mrs Alexander   I heard about it yesterday. Dreadful. Dreadful.

Christopher   Do you know who killed him?

Mrs Alexander   No, I don't.

Christopher   Somebody must know because the person who killed Wellington knows that they killed Wellington. Unless they were a mad person and didn't know what they were doing. Or unless they had amnesia.

Mrs Alexander   Well I suppose you're probably right.

Christopher   Thank you for helping me with my investigation.

Mrs Alexander   You're Christopher aren't you?

Christopher   Yes. I live at number 36.

Mrs Alexander   We haven't talked before, have we?

Christopher   No. I don't talk to strangers. But I'm doing detective work.

Mrs Alexander   I see you every day, going to school on your school bus. It's very nice of you to come and say hello. Even if it's only because you're doing detective work.

Christopher   Thank you.

Mrs Alexander   I have a grandson your age.

Christopher   My age is fifteen years and three months and three days.

Mrs Alexander   Well almost your age. You don't have a dog, do you?

Christopher   No.

Mrs Alexander   You'd probably like a dog wouldn't you?

Christopher   I have a rat.

Mrs Alexander   A rat?

Christopher   He's called Toby.

Mrs Alexander   Oh.

Christopher   Most people don't like rats because they think they carry diseases like bubonic plague. But that's only because they lived in sewers and stowed away on ships coming from foreign countries where there were strange diseases. But rats are very clean.

Mrs Alexander   Do you want to come in for tea?

Christopher   I don't go into other people's houses.

Mrs Alexander   Well maybe I could bring some tea out here. Do you like lemon squash?

Christopher   I only like orange squash.

Mrs Alexander   Luckily I have some of that as well. And what about Battenberg?

Christopher   I don't know because I don't know what Battenberg is.

Mrs Alexander   It's a kind of cake. It has marzipan icing round the edge.

Christopher   Is it a long cake with a square cross-section which is divided into equally sized, alternately coloured squares?

Mrs Alexander   Yes I think you could probably describe it like that.

Christopher   I think I'd like the pink squares but not the yellow squares because I don't like yellow. And I don't know what marzipan is so I don't know whether I'll like that.

Mrs Alexander   I'm afraid marzipan is yellow too. Perhaps I should bring out some biscuits instead. Do you like biscuits?

Christopher   Yes. Some sorts of biscuits.

Mrs Alexander   I'll get a selection.

She goes into her house.

He waits. Then before she gets back.

Siobhan   She moved very slowly because she was an old lady and she was inside the house for more than six minutes and I began to get nervous because I didn't know her well enough to know whether she was telling the truth about getting orange squash and Battenberg cake. And I thought she might be ringing the police and then I'd get into much more serious trouble because of the caution. So I walked away.

The **Company** *cheer, as if a goal has been scored.*

Christopher   Why would you kill a dog?

Siobhan   I wouldn't.

Christopher   I think you would only kill a dog if a) you hated the dog or b) if you were mad or c) because you wanted to make Mrs Shears upset. I don't know anybody who hated Wellington so if it was a) it was probably a stranger. I don't know any mad people either, so if it was b) it was also probably a stranger.

Siobhan   Right.

Christopher   But most murders are committed by someone who is known to the victim. In fact, you are most likely to be murdered by a member of your own family on Christmas Day.

Siobhan   Is that a fact?

Christopher   Yes actually it is a fact. Wellington was therefore most likely to have been killed by someone known to him. I only know one person who didn't like Mrs Shears and that is Mr Shears who divorced Mrs Shears and left her to live somewhere else and who knew Wellington very well indeed. This means that Mr Shears is my Prime Suspect.

Siobhan   Christopher.

Christopher   I am going to find out more about Mr Shears.

Mrs Gascoyne   Mr Boone, nobody has ever taken an A level in the school before.

Ed   He can be the first then.

Mrs Gascoyne   I don't know if we have the facilities in the school to allow him to do that.

Ed   Then get the facilities.

Mrs Gascoyne   I can't treat Christopher differently to any other student.

Ed   Why not?

Mrs Gascoyne   Because then everybody would want to be treated differently.

Ed   So?

Mrs Gascoyne   It would set a precedent. Christopher can always do his A levels later. When he's 18.

Ed   Christopher is getting a crap enough deal already don't you think, without you shitting on him from a great height as well. Jesus, this is the one thing he's really good at.

Mrs Gascoyne   We should talk about this later. Maybe on our own.

Ed   Are there things which you're too embarrassed to say to me in front of Christopher?

Mrs Gascoyne   No. It's not that.

Ed   Say them now then.

Mrs Gascoyne   If Christopher sits an A level then he would have to have a member of staff looking after him on his own in a separate room.

Ed   I'll pay for it. They can do it after school. Here. Fifty quid. Is that enough?

Mrs Gascoyne   Mr Boone.

Ed   I'm not going to take no for an answer.

Ed *turns to* **Christopher**.

Ed   Where have you been?

Christopher   I have been out.

Ed   I have just had a phone call from Mrs Shears. What the hell were you doing poking round her garden?

Christopher   I was doing detective work trying to figure out who killed Wellington.

Ed   How many times do I have to tell you Christopher? I told you to keep your nose out of other people's business.

Christopher   I think Mr Shears probably killed Wellington.

Ed (*shouts*)   I will not have that man's name mentioned in my house.

Beat.

Everybody on stage pauses to look at **Ed** *and* **Christopher**.

Christopher   Why not?

Ed   That man is evil.

Christopher   Does that mean he might have killed Wellington?

Ed   Jesus wept.

Christopher   I know you told me not to get involved in other people's business but Mrs Shears is a friend of ours.

Ed   Well, she's not a friend any more.

Christopher   Why not?

Ed   OK Christopher. I am going to say this for the last and final time. I will not tell you again. Look at me when I'm talking to you for God's sake. Look at me. You are not to go asking Mrs Shears who killed that bloody dog. You are not to go asking anyone who killed that bloody dog. You are not to go trespassing on other people's gardens. You are to stop this ridiculous bloody detective game right now. I am going to make you promise me Christopher. And you know what it means when I make you promise.

Christopher   I know.

Ed   Promise me that you will give up this ridiculous game right now, OK?

Christopher   I promise.

Siobhan   I think I would make a very good astronaut.

Ed   Yes mate. You probably would.

Siobhan   To be a good astronaut you have to be intelligent and I'm intelligent. You also have to understand how machines work and I'm good at understanding how machines work.

Christopher   You also have to be someone who would like being on their own in a tiny spacecraft thousands and thousands of miles away from the surface of the earth and not panic or get claustrophobia or homesick or insane. And I really like little spaces so long as there is no one else in them with me.

Ed   I noticed.

Siobhan   Sometimes when I want to be on my own I get into the airing cupboard and slide in beside the boiler and pull the door closed behind me and sit there and think for hours and it makes me feel very calm.

Christopher   So I would have to be an astronaut on my own or have my own part of the spacecraft that no one else could come into. And also there are no yellow things or brown things in a spacecraft so that would be OK, too.

And I would have to talk to other people from Mission Control, but we would do that through a radio link-up and a TV monitor so it wouldn't be like real people who are strangers but it would be like playing a computer game.

Ed   Which you like.

Christopher   Also I wouldn't be homesick at all because I'd be surrounded by lots of things I like, which are machines and computers and outer space. And I would be able to look out of a little window in the spacecraft and know that there was no one else near me for thousands and thousands –

Ed   Christopher.

Christopher   What?

Ed   Could you please, just, give it a bit of a break, mate. Please.

Siobhan   And know that there was no one else near me for thousands and thousands of miles which is what I sometimes pretend at night in the summer when I go and lie on the lawn and look up at the sky and I put my hands round the sides of my face so that I can't see the fence and the chimney and the washing line and I can pretend I'm in space.

And all I could see would be stars. And stars are the places where the molecules that life is made of were constructed billions of years ago. For example, all the iron in your blood, which stops you being anaemic, was made in a star.

And I would like it if I could take Toby with me into space, and that might be allowed because they sometimes do take animals into space for experiments, so if I could think of a good experiment you could do with a rat that didn't hurt the rat, I could make them let me take Toby.

But if they didn't let me I would still go because it would be a Dream Come True.

Christopher   Father said.

Siobhan   I see that's a pity.

Christopher   So the book is finished.

Siobhan   Well, Christopher, if your father said he wanted you to stop then I think he probably has a good reason and I think you should stop. But you can still be very proud because what you've written so far is just, well it's great.

Christopher   It's very short.

Siobhan   Well some very good books are very short.

Christopher   / It's not a proper book.

Siobhan   Why not?

Christopher   It doesn't have a proper ending. I never found out who killed Wellington. So the murderer is still At Large.

Siobhan   Not all murders are solved Christopher. Not all murderers are caught.

Christopher   I don't like the idea that he could be living somewhere nearby and that I might meet him when I go out for a walk at night.

Siobhan   I don't think that's going to happen Christopher.

Christopher   Father said I was never to mention Mr Shears' name in our house again and that he was an evil man and maybe that meant he was the person who killed Wellington.

Siobhan   Christopher, I think you should do what your father tells you to do.

Mrs Alexander   What happened to you the other day?

Christopher   Which day?

Mrs Alexander   I came out again and you'd gone. I had to eat all the biscuits myself.

Christopher   I went away.

Mrs Alexander   I gathered that.

Christopher   I thought you might ring the police.

Mrs Alexander   Why on earth would I do that?

Christopher   Because I was poking my nose into other people's business and Father said I shouldn't investigate who killed Wellington. And a policeman gave me a caution and if I get into trouble again it will be a lot worse because of the caution.

Mrs Alexander   You're very shy aren't you Christopher?

Christopher   I'm not allowed to talk to you.

Mrs Alexander   Don't worry I'm not going to tell the police and I'm not going to tell your father because there's nothing wrong with having a chat. Having a chat is just being friendly, isn't it?

Christopher   I don't do chatting.

Mrs Alexander   Do you like computers?

Christopher   Yes. I like computers. I have a computer at home in my bedroom.

Mrs Alexander   I know. I can see you sitting at your computer in your bedroom sometimes when I look across the street.

Christopher   And I like maths and looking after Toby. And I also like outer space and I like being on my own.

Mrs Alexander   I bet you're very good at Maths aren't you?

Christopher   I am. I'm going to do A level Maths next month. And I'm going to get an A*.

Mrs Alexander   Really? A level maths?

Christopher   Yes. I don't tell lies.

Mrs Alexander   I apologise. I didn't mean to suggest that you were lying. I just wondered if I heard you correctly. I'm a little deaf sometimes.

Christopher   I remember you told me. I'm the first person to do an A level from my school because it's a special school. All the other children at my school are stupid. Except I'm not meant to call them stupid, even though that is what they are.

Mrs Alexander   Well I am very impressed. And I hope you do get an A*.

Christopher   I will.

Mrs Alexander   And the other thing I know about you is your favourite colour is not yellow.

Christopher   No. And it's not brown either. My favourite colour is red and metal colour. Do you know Mr Shears?

Mrs Alexander   Not really, no. I mean I knew him well enough to say hello but I didn't know much about him. I think he worked in the National Westminster bank in town.

Christopher   Father said that he is an evil man. Do you know why he said that?

Mrs Alexander   Perhaps it would be best not to talk about these things Christopher.

Christopher   Why not?

Mrs Alexander   Because maybe your father is right and you shouldn't go round asking questions about this.

Christopher   Why?

Mrs Alexander   Because obviously he is going to find it quite upsetting.

Christopher   Why is he going to find it quite upsetting?

Mrs Alexander   I think you know why your father doesn't like Mr Shears very much.

Christopher   Did Mr Shears kill Mother?

Mrs Alexander   Kill her?

Christopher   Yes. Did he kill Mother?

Mrs Alexander   No. No. Of course he didn't kill your mother.

Christopher   But did he give her stress so that she died of a heart attack?

Mrs Alexander   I honestly don't know what you're talking about, Christopher.

Christopher   Or did he hurt her so that she had to go into hospital?

Mrs Alexander   Did she have to go into hospital?

Christopher   Yes. And it wasn't very serious at first but she had a heart attack when she was in hospital.

Mrs Alexander   Oh my goodness.

Christopher   And she died.

Mrs Alexander   Oh my goodness. Oh Christopher I am so, so sorry. I never realised.

Christopher   Why did you say 'I think you know why your father doesn't like Mr Shears very much?'

Mrs Alexander   Oh dear, dear, dear. So you don't know?

Christopher   Don't know what?

Mrs Alexander   Christopher look, perhaps we should take a little walk in the park together. This is not the place to be talking about this kind of thing.

Mrs Alexander   I am going to say something to you and you must promise not to tell your father that I told you this.

Christopher   Why?

Mrs Alexander   I shouldn't have said what I said. And if I don't explain, you'll carry on wondering what I meant. And you might ask your father. And I don't want you to do that because I don't want you to upset him. But you have to promise not to tell anyone I said this to you.

Christopher   Why?

Mrs Alexander   Christopher, please, just trust me.

Christopher   I promise.

Mrs Alexander   Your mother before she died was very good friends with Mr Shears.

Christopher   I know.

Mrs Alexander   No Christopher, I'm not sure that you do. I mean that they were very good friends. Very, very good friends.

Christopher   Do you mean that they were doing sex?

Mrs Alexander   Yes, Christopher, that is what I mean.

I'm sorry Christopher. I really didn't mean to say anything that was going to upset you.

Christopher   Was that why Mr Shears left Mrs Shears, because he was doing sex with someone else when he was married to Mrs Shears.

Mrs Alexander   Yes. I expect so.

Christopher   I think I should go now.

Mrs Alexander   Are you OK Christopher?

Christopher   I can't be on my own with you because you are a stranger.

Mrs Alexander   I'm not a stranger Christopher, I'm a friend.

Ed   And what have you been up to, young man?

Christopher   I went to the shop to get some liquorice laces and a Milky Bar.

Ed   You were a long time.

Christopher   I talked to Mrs Alexander's dog outside the shop. And stroked him and he sniffed my trousers.

Rhodri   God you do get the third degree, don't you? So how are you doing captain?

Christopher   I'm doing very well, thank you Rhodri.

Rhodri   What's 251 times 864?

Christopher   216,864. Is that right?

Rhodri   I haven't got a bloody clue.

Ed   I'll stick one of these aloo gobi sag things in the oven for you, OK?

Christopher   OK.

Rhodri   With your little bottle of red paint in it, eh Christopher?

Christopher   It's not red paint it's red food colouring because I don't eat yellow food. If you put red paint into a curry it would be extremely dangerous and it would probably kill you.

Ed   Ha! Rodders! You Plonker!

Ed *laughs at* **Rhodri**, **Rhodri** *leaves*.

Ed *finds* **Christopher**'s *book on the kitchen table.*

Siobhan   Have you told your father about this?

Christopher   No.

Siobhan   Are you going to tell your father about this?

Christopher   No.

Ed *goes to the book.*

There is a tone.

He begins reading **Christopher**'s *book.*

Siobhan   Did it make you sad to find this out?

Christopher   Find what out?

Siobhan   Did it make you sad to find out that your mother and Mr Shears had an affair?

Christopher   No.

Siobhan   Are you telling the truth Christopher?

Christopher   I always tell the truth. I don't feel sad about it because Mother is dead and because Mr Shears isn't around any more. So I would be feeling sad about something that isn't real and doesn't exist and that would be stupid.

Siobhan   What was your mother like Christopher?

Do you remember much about her?

Christopher   I remember 20 July 2006. I was 9 years old. It was a Saturday. We were on holiday in Cornwall. We were on the beach in a place called Polperro. Mother was wearing a pair of shorts made out of denim and a stripey blue swimming costume and she was smoking cigarettes called Consulate, which were mint flavour. And she wasn't swimming. She was sunbathing on a towel, which had red and purple stripes, and she was reading a book by Georgette Heyer called *The Masqueraders*. And then she finished sunbathing and went into the water and she said

Judy   Bloody Nora it's cold.

Christopher   'Bloody Nora it's cold.' And she said I should come and swim too, but I didn't like swimming because I don't like taking my clothes off. And she said I should just roll up my trousers and walk into the water a little way. So I did. And Mother said

Judy   Christopher! Christopher! Over here love. Christopher! Look it's lovely.

Christopher   And she jumped backwards and disappeared under the water and I thought a shark had eaten her and I screamed. And she stood up out of the water again and came over to where I was standing and held up her right hand and spread out her fingers like a fan.

Judy   Come on Christopher, touch my hand. Come on now. Stop screaming. Touch my hand. Listen to me Christopher. You can do it. It's OK Christopher. It's OK. There aren't any sharks in Cornwall.

Ed   When we were inside the park Mrs Alexander stopped walking and said 'I am going to say something to you and you must promise not to tell your father that I told you this.

Your mother before she died was very good friends with Mr
Shears.'

Christopher   And other times she used to say:

Judy   If I hadn't married your father I think I'd be living in
a little farmhouse in the South of France with someone
called Jean. And he'd be, ooh, a local handyman. You know,
doing painting and decorating for people, gardening,
building fences. And we'd have a veranda with figs growing
over it and there would be a field of sunflowers at the bottom
of the garden and a little town on the hill in the distance and
we'd sit outside in the evening and drink red wine and
smoke Gauloise cigarettes and watch the sun go down.

Ed   What is this?

Christopher *looks at* **Ed**.

Christopher   It's a book I'm writing.

Ed   Is this true? Did you speak to Mrs Alexander?

Christopher   Yes.

Ed   Jesus, Christopher, how stupid are you? What the fuck
did I tell you Christopher?

Christopher   Not to mention Mr Shears name in the house.
And not to go asking Mrs Shears, or anyone about who
killed that bloody dog. And not to go trespassing on other
people's gardens. And to stop this bloody ridiculous
detective game. Except I haven't done any of those things. I
just asked Mrs Alexander about Mr Shears because . . .

Ed   Don't give me that bollocks you little shit. You knew
exactly what you were bloody doing. I've read the book,
remember. What else did I say Christopher?

Christopher   I don't know.

Ed   Come on you're the memory man. Not to go round sticking your fucking nose into other people's business. And what do you do? You go around sticking your nose into other people's business. You go around raking up the past and sharing it with every Tom, Dick and Harry you bump into. What am I going to do with you Christopher? What the fuck am I going to do with you?

Ed *throws* **Christopher***'s book.*

Christopher   I was just chatting with Mrs Alexander. I wasn't doing investigating.

Ed   I ask you to do one thing for me, Christopher. One thing.

Christopher   I didn't want to talk to Mrs Alexander. It was Mrs Alexander who . . .

Ed *grabs* **Christopher***'s arm.*

Christopher *screams.*

They fight each other.

Ed *shakes* **Christopher** *hard with both hands.*

Christopher *falls unconscious for a few seconds.*

Ed *stands above him.*

Ed   I need a drink.

He goes and picks up the book.

He leaves.

He comes back without the book.

Ed   I'm sorry I hit you.

I didn't mean to.

I love you very much Christopher. Don't ever forget that. I know I lose my rag occasionally. And I know I shouldn't. But I only do it because I worry about you, because I don't want to see you getting into trouble, because I don't want you to get hurt. Do you understand?

Christopher   Where's my book?

Ed   Christopher, do you understand that I love you?

Ed *holds his right hand up and spreads his fingers out in a fan.*
Christopher *does the same with his left hand. They make their
fingers and thumbs touch each other.*

Christopher   Is it in the dustbin at the front of the house?

Siobhan   Christopher, why have you got a bruise on the
side of your face?

Christopher   Father was angry. He grabbed me so I hit him
and then we had a fight.

Siobhan   Did he grab you hard?

Christopher   Yes.

Siobhan   Christopher, are you frightened of going home?

Christopher   No. Because I need to find my book.

Siobhan   Do you want to talk about it any more?

Christopher   No. Because grabbing is OK if it's on your
arm or your shoulder when you are angry, but you can't
grab someone's hair or their face. But hitting is not allowed,
except if you are already in a fight with someone then it is
not so bad.

Siobhan   When I got home from school Father was still at
work so I went outside and looked inside the dustbin.

But the book wasn't there.

I wondered if Father had put it into his van and driven to
the tip and put it into one of the big bins there but I did not
want that to be true because then I would never see it again.
One other possibility was that Father had hidden my book
somewhere in the house. So I decided to do some detecting
and see if I could find it.

I started by looking in the kitchen.

Then I detected in the utility room.

Then I detected in the dining room.

Then I detected in the living room where I found the missing wheel from my Airfix Saturn 1b Rocket 172 model under the sofa.

Then I went upstairs but I didn't do any detecting in my own room because I reasoned that Father wouldn't hide something from me in my own room unless he was being very clever and doing what is called a Double Bluff like in a real murder mystery novel, so I decided to look in my own room only if I couldn't find the book anywhere else.

I detected in the bathroom, but the only place to look was in the airing cupboard and there was nothing in there.

Which meant the only room left to detect in was Father's bedroom.

I started by looking under the bed.

There were seven shoes and a comb with lots of hair in it and a monkey wrench and a chocolate biscuit and a magazine called *Men Only* and a pair of navy underpants from Marks & Spencer that are called Y fronts and a Homer Simpson pattern tie and a wooden spoon, but not my book. Then I looked in the drawers on either side of the dressing table. But these only contained aspirin and nail clippers and batteries and dental floss and tissues and a spare false tooth and a tampon but my book wasn't there either.

Then I looked in his clothes cupboard. In the bottom of the cupboard was a large plastic toolbox which was full of tools for doing-it-yourself but I could see these without opening the box because it was made of transparent grey plastic. Then I saw that there was another box underneath the toolbox.

The other box was an old cardboard box that is called a shirt box because people used to buy shirts in them.

Christopher *finds these things including, finally, the shirt box.*

Siobhan   And when I opened the shirt box I saw my book was inside it.

Christopher *finds his book.*

Siobhan   Then I heard his van pulling up outside the house and I knew that I had to think fast and be clever.

I heard Father shutting the door of the van.

And that is when I saw the envelope.

It was an envelope addressed to me and it was lying under my book in the shirt box with some other envelopes. I picked it up.

Christopher *finds the envelope.*

Siobhan   It had never been opened.

It said

Judy   Christopher Boone, 36 Randolph Street, Swindon, Wiltshire.

Siobhan   Then I noticed there were lots of envelopes and they were all addressed to me. And this was interesting and confusing.

And then I noticed how the words Christopher and Swindon were written. They were written like this.

Judy   Christopher. Swindon.

Siobhan   I only know three people who do little circles instead of dots over the letter i. And one of them is Siobhan. And one of them was Mr Loxley who used to teach at the school. And one of them was Mother.

Ed   Christopher?

Christopher   Hello.

Ed   So what have you been up to young man?

Christopher   Today we did Life Skills with Siobhan. Which was Using Money and Public Transport. And I had tomato soup for lunch and three apples. And I practised some maths in the afternoon and we went for a walk in the park with Mrs Peters and collected leaves for making collages.

Ed   Excellent, excellent. What do you fancy for chow tonight?

Christopher   Baked beans and broccoli.

Ed   I think that can be very easily arranged.

I'm just going to put those shelves up in the living room if that's all right with you. I'll make a bit of a racket I'm afraid so if you want to watch television we're going to have to shift it upstairs.

Christopher   I'll go and be on my own in my room.

Ed   Good man.

Siobhan   I went up to my room. And when I was in the room I shut the door and took out the envelope. I opened the envelope. Inside there was a letter. And this was what was written in the letter.

Judy   451c Chapter Road, Willesden, London NW2 5NG. 020 8887 8907. Dear Christopher. I'm sorry it's been such a very long time since I wrote my last letter to you. I've been very busy. I've got a new job working as a secretary for a factory that makes things out of steel. You'd like it a lot. The factory is full of huge machines that make the steel and cut it and bend it into whatever shapes they need. Also we've moved into a new flat at last as you can see from the address. It's not as nice as the old one and I don't like Willesden very much, but it's easier for Roger to get to work and he's bought it (he only rented the other one) so we can get our own furniture and paint the walls the colour we want to. You haven't written to me yet, so I know that you are probably still angry with me. I'm sorry Christopher. But I still love you. I hope you don't stay angry with me for ever. And I'd love it if you were able to write me a letter (but remember to send it to the new address!).

I think about you all the time.

Lots of love,

Your Mum.

Siobhan   I was really confused. Mother had never worked as a secretary for a factory that made things out of steel. And Mother had never lived in London. And Mother had never written a letter to me before.

There was no date on the letter so I couldn't work out when Mother had written the letter and then I looked at the front of the envelope and I saw there was a postmark and there was a date on the postmark, 16 October 2011, which meant that the letter was posted eighteen months after Mother had died.

Ed   What are you doing?

Christopher   I'm reading a letter.

Ed   I've finished the drilling. That David Attenborough nature programme's on telly if you're interested.

Christopher   OK.

Ed *leaves*.

Siobhan   When I started writing my book there was only one mystery to solve. Now there were two. Perhaps the letter was in the wrong envelope and it had been written before Mother had died. Perhaps it wasn't a letter from Mother. Perhaps it was a letter to another person called Christopher from that Christopher's mother. Perhaps someone else had written the letter and pretended to be Mother.

I decided that I would not think about it anymore that night because I didn't have enough information and could easily LEAP TO THE WRONG CONCLUSIONS.

Christopher *lies down on the floor. He curls himself up into a ball.*

Night falls. Morning rises.

The next day **Christopher** *comes home from school.*

Ed   You're soaking.

Christopher   Yes.

Ed   Give me your coat I'll hang it up.

How was school?

Christopher   It was good thank you.

Joseph Fleming took his trousers off and went to the toilet all over the floor of the changing room and started to eat it, but Mr Davis stopped him.

Ed   Good old Mr Davis eh?

Christopher   Joseph eats everything.

Ed   Does he?

Christopher   He once ate one of the little blocks of blue disinfectant, which hang inside the toilets. And he once ate a £50 note from his mother's wallet. And he eats string and rubber bands and tissues and writing paper and paints and plastic forks. Also he bangs his chin and screams a lot.

Ed   I know how he feels. Christopher –

Christopher   Tyrone said that there was a horse and a pig in the poo so I said he was being stupid, but Siobhan said he wasn't. They were small plastic animals from the library that the staff use to make people tell stories. And Joseph had eaten them.

Ed   Christopher I've got to go out.

Christopher   Why?

Ed   I've just had a call there's a lady. Her cellar has flooded. I've got to go out and fix it.

Christopher   Is it an emergency?

Ed   Yes mate.

Christopher   Why can't Rhodri go?

Ed   He's already out on a call.

Christopher   So there are two emergencies.

Ed   That's right mate.

Christopher   It is raining very heavily.

Ed   It is.

Christopher   The rain looks like white sparks.

Ed   Christopher if I go out will you be OK?

Christopher   Yes I will because there's no one around because everybody's staying in doors.

Ed   Good. Good. Good. Good lad.

Christopher   I like looking at the rain.

Ed   Terrific.

Christopher   I like it because it makes me think how all the water in the world is connected.

Ed   I'll have my mobile with me.

Christopher   Yes.

Ed   So you can call me if there's a problem.

Christopher   Yes.

Ed   Behave yourself Christopher yeah?

Christopher   Yes.

Ed *exits*.

Siobhan   So I went into his bedroom and opened up the cupboard and lifted the toolbox off the top of the shirt box and opened the shirt box. I counted out the letters. There were forty-three of them. They were all addressed to me in the same handwriting. I took one and opened it. Inside was this letter.

*As **Judy** reads so **Christopher** begins to assemble his train set. His building becomes frantic. At times almost balletic.*

Judy   451c Chapter Road London NW2 5NG 020 8887 8907. I was looking through some old photos last night, which made me sad. Then I found a photo of you playing with the train set we bought for you a couple of Christmases ago. And that made me happy because it was one of the really good times we had together. Do you remember how you played with it all day and you refused to go to bed at night because you were still playing with it. We told you about train timetables and you made a train timetable. And there was a little wooden station, too, and we showed you how people who wanted to go on the train went to the station and bought a ticket and then got on a train? And you played with it for weeks and weeks and weeks. I liked remembering that a lot.

Siobhan   Then I opened another envelope. This was the letter that was inside.

Christopher *continues to build a train set. It should be as big as he can possibly make it. He makes it with attention and detail as the letter continues.*

Judy   Dear Christopher. I said that I wanted to explain to you why I went away when I had the time to do it properly. Now I have lots of time. So I'm sitting on the sofa here with this letter and the radio on and I'm going to try and explain.

I was not a very good mother Christopher. Maybe if things had been different, maybe if you'd been different, I might have been better at it. But that's just the way things turned out.

I'm not like your father. Your father is a much more patient person. He just gets on with things and if things upset him he doesn't let it show.

But that's not the way I am and there's nothing I can do to change it.

Do you remember once when we were shopping in town together? And we went into Bentalls and it was really crowded and we had to get a Christmas present for Grandma? And you were frightened because of all the people in the shop. It was the middle of Christmas shopping when everyone was in town. And I was talking to Mr Land who works on the kitchen floor and went to school with me. And you crouched down on the floor and put your hands over your ears and you were in the way of everyone so I got cross because I don't like shopping at Christmas either, and I told you to behave and I tried to pick you up and move you. But you shouted and you knocked those mixers off the shelf and there was a big crash. And everyone turned round to see what was going on and Mr Land was really nice about it but there were boxes and bits of string and bits of broken bowl on the floor and everyone was staring and I saw that you had wet yourself and I was so cross and I wanted to take you out of the shop but you wouldn't let me touch you and you just lay on the floor and screamed and banged your hands and feet on the floor and the manager came and asked me what the problem was and I was at the end of my tether and I had to pay for two broken mixers and we just had to wait until you stopped screaming. And then I had to walk you all the way home, which took hours because I knew you wouldn't go on the bus again.

And I remember that night I just cried and cried and cried and your father was really nice about it at first and he made you supper and put you to bed and he said these things happen and it would be OK. But I said I couldn't take it anymore and eventually he got really cross and he told me I was being stupid and said I should pull myself together and I hit him, which was wrong, but I was so upset.

We had a lot of arguments like that.

Because I often thought I couldn't take it any more. And your father is really patient, but I'm not. I get cross, even though I don't mean to. And by the end we stopped talking to each other very much because we knew it would always end up in an argument. And I felt really lonely.

Siobhan   And that was when I started spending lots of time with Roger.

Judy   And that was when I started spending lots of time with Roger.

And I know you might not understand any of this, but I wanted to try to explain so that you knew.

Siobhan   We had a lot in common. And then we realised that we were in love with one ano –

Judy   I said that I couldn't leave you and he was sad about that but he understood that you were really important to me.

Siobhan   And you started to shout and I got cross and I threw the food across the room. Which I know I shouldn't have done.

Judy   You grabbed the chopping board and you threw it and it hit my foot and broke my toes.

Siobhan   And afterwards at home your father and I had a huge argument.

Judy   And I couldn't walk properly for a month, do you remember and your father had to look after you.

Siobhan   And I remember looking at the two of you and seeing you together and thinking how you were really different with him. Much calmer.

Judy   And it made me so sad because it was like you didn't need me at all.

Siobhan   And I think then I realised you and your father were probably better off if I wasn't living in the house.

Judy   And Roger asked me if I wanted to come with him.

Siobhan   And it broke my heart but eventually I decided it would be better for all of us if I went.

Judy   And so I said yes.

Siobhan   And I meant to say goodbye.

Judy   But when I rang your father he said I couldn't –

He was really angry. He said I couldn't –

Siobhan   He said I couldn't talk to you.

Judy   And I didn't know what to do.

Siobhan   He said I was being selfish and that I was never to set foot inside the house again.

Judy   And so I haven't.

Siobhan   I wonder if you can understand any of this. I know it will be difficult for you.

Judy   I thought what I was doing was the best for all of us. I hope it is.

Siobhan   Christopher I never meant to hurt you.

Judy   I used to have dreams that everything would get better. Do you remember you used to say that you wanted to be an astronaut? Well I used to have dreams where you were an astronaut and you were on television and I thought that's my son. I wonder what it is that you want to be now. Has it changed? Are you still doing maths? I hope you are.

Judy   Loads and loads of love, Mother.

Christopher *moves to the middle of the track. He crouches down. He rolls himself into a ball. He starts hitting his hands and his feet and his head against the floor as the letter continues. His thrashing has exhausted him. He has been sick. He lies still for a while, wrapped in a ball.*

Ed   Christopher? Christopher?

Christopher *doesn't respond.*

Ed   Christopher, Christopher what the hell are you doing? What are you? These are. Oh shit. Oh Christ.

Christopher *doesn't move or respond.*

Ed *stops himself from crying.*

Ed   It was an accident.

Christopher *doesn't respond.*

Ed   I don't know what to say . . . I was in such a mess . . . I said she was in hospital . . . because I didn't know how to explain it was so complicated. And once I'd said that . . .

I couldn't change it. It just . . . It got out of control.

Christopher *doesn't respond.*

After a time **Ed** *approaches him.*

Very, very gently he touches his shoulder. **Christopher** *doesn't respond.*

Oh Jesus, Christopher. You've got sick all over your . . .

Ed   Let's sit you up and get your clothes off and get you into bed OK? I'm going to have to touch you, but it's going to be all right.

Ed *lifts* **Christopher** *onto the side of the bed.* **Christopher** *doesn't resist or fight at all.*

Ed *takes* **Christopher**'s *jumper and shirt off.*

Ed   Have you had anything to eat this evening?

Can I get you anything to eat Christopher?

OK. Look. I'm going to go and put your clothes into the washing machine and then I'll come back, OK?

Ed *moves away.* **Christopher** *sits alone.* **Ed** *comes back.*

Ed   How are you feeling? Can I get you anything?

Look maybe I shouldn't say this, but . . . I want you to know that you can trust me . . . You have to know that I am going to tell you the truth from now on. About everything. Because . . . if you don't tell the truth now, then later on it hurts even more. So . . . I killed Wellington, Christopher. Just . . . let me explain. When your mum left . . . Eileen . . . Mrs Shears . . . she was very good to me. She helped me through a very difficult time. Well, you know how she was round here most days. I thought . . . Well . . . Shit Christopher, I'm trying to keep this simple . . . I thought she might carry on coming over . . . I thought . . . and maybe I was being stupid . . . I thought she might . . . eventually . . . want to move in here. Or that we might move into her house. I thought we were friends. And I guess I thought wrong. We argued Christopher, and . . . She said some things I'm not going to say to you because they're not nice . . . I think she cared more for that bloody dog than for us. And maybe that's not so stupid looking back. Maybe it's easier living on your own looking after some stupid mutt, than sharing your life with other actual human beings. I mean, shit, buddy we're not exactly low maintenance, are we? Anyway, we had this row. And after this particularly nasty little blow-out, she chucked me out of the house. And you know what that bloody dog was like. Nice as pie one moment, roll over, tickle its stomach. Sink its teeth into your leg the next. Anyway, we're yelling at each other and it's in the garden. So when she slams the door behind me the bugger's waiting for me. And . . . I know, I know. Maybe if I'd just given it a kick it would probably have backed off. But, shit Christopher, when the red mist comes down . . . Christ, you know what I'm talking about. I mean we're not that different me and you. And it was like everything I'd been bottling up for two years just . . .

I never meant for it to turn out like this.

Ed *holds his right hand up for* **Christopher** *to touch.*

Christopher *ignores it.* **Ed** *stares at* **Christopher**.

Ed   OK. Look. Christopher. I'm sorry. Let's leave it for tonight, OK? I'm going to go downstairs and you get some sleep and we'll talk in the morning. It's going to be all right. Honestly. Trust me.

Ed *leaves.* **Christopher** *groans. He starts counting.*

Christopher   2, 4, 8, 16, 32, 64, 128, 256, 512, 1024, 2048, 4096, 8192, 16384, 32, 768, 32, 768, 32, 768 –

Siobhan   Father had murdered Wellington. That meant he could murder me.

I had to get out of the house.

I made a decision. I did this by thinking of all the things I could do and deciding whether they were the right decision or not.

Ed   Stay home.

Siobhan   I decided I couldn't stay home any more

Ed   Christopher, please.

Christopher   No because I can't live in the house with you any more because it is dangerous.

I can't go and live with you because you can't look after me when school's closed.

Siobhan   I could try and –

Christopher   No because you're a teacher.

Siobhan   Yes.

Christopher   Not a friend or a member of my family.

Uncle Terry   You could go and live with your Uncle Terry.

Christopher   You live in Sunderland. I don't know how to get to Sunderland.

Uncle Terry   Get a train. Get the train from Swindon.

Christopher   And you smoke cigarettes. And you stroke my hair.

You're not a friend either.

Mrs Alexander   I think I am a friend.

Christopher   No. And you're not a member of my family.

Mrs Alexander   I do have a dog.

Chistopher   Yes but I can't stay overnight in your house or use your toilet because you've used it and you're a stranger.

Mrs Alexander   I'm not really a stranger Christopher.

Christopher   Yes.

Judy   451c Chapter Road, London NW2 5NG.

451c Chapter Road, London NW2 5NG.

451c Chapter Road, London NW2 5NG.

Christopher *looks at* **Judy**.

451c Chapter Road.

Christopher   London NW2 5NG.

Light falls.

Part Two

*The **Company** is on stage.*

Siobhan   Christopher I want to ask you something. Mrs Gascoyne wondered if we would like to do a play this year. She asked me to ask everybody if we'd like to make some kind of performance for the school. Everybody could join in and play a part in it.

Mrs Gascoyne   I think it would be a good thing for everybody to join in and play a part in it.

Siobhan   I was wondering if you'd like to make a play out of your book.

Christopher   No.

Siobhan   I think it could be really good fun Christopher.

Mrs Gascoyne   I think it could be really good fun.

Christopher   No. It's a book and its for me and not everybody just for me.

Siobhan   I know that Christopher but I think a lot of people would be interested in what would happen if people took your book and started acting bits out of it.

Christopher   No. I don't like acting because it is pretending that something is real when it is not really real at all so it is like a kind of lie.

Siobhan   But people like stories Christopher. Some people find things which are kind of true in things which are made up. You like your Sherlock Holmes stories and you know Sherlock Holmes isn't a real person don't you?

I would help you if you were worried about that.

Christopher   No.

Reverend Peters   I think I'd rather like to take the part of a policeman.

Christopher   You're too old to be a policeman.

Ed (*shouting*)   Christopher. Christopher.

Company *move into the space and watch* **Ed**.

Christopher *hides*.

Nobody gives **Ed** *a clue as to where* **Christopher** *is.*

After a while he gives up.

Then **Christopher** *comes out. He is holding* **Toby** *in his cage.*

Mrs Alexander   Christopher, what on earth has happened to you?

Christopher   Can you look after Toby for me?

Mrs Alexander   Who's Toby?

Christopher   Toby's my pet rat.

Mrs Alexander   Oh . . . Oh yes. I remember now. You told me.

Christopher   He eats special pellets and you can buy them from a pet shop. And he needs new water in his bottle every day, too.

Mrs Alexander   Why do you need somebody to look after Toby, Christopher?

Christopher   I'm going to London.

Mrs Alexander   How long are you going for?

Christopher   Until I go to university.

Mrs Alexander   Right. Are you and your father moving house?

Christopher   No.

Mrs Alexander   So, why are you going to London?

Christopher   I'm going to live with Mother.

Mrs Alexander   I thought you told me your mother was dead.

Christopher   I thought she was dead but she was still alive. And Father lied to me. And also he killed Wellington and so that means that he could kill me.

Mrs Alexander   Is your mother here?

Christopher   No. Mother is in London. She lives at 451c Chapter Road, London NW2 5NG.

Mrs Alexander   So you're going to London on your own?

Christopher   I think I am going to do that yes.

Mrs Alexander   Look, Christopher, why don't you come inside and sit down and we can talk about this.

Christopher   No. I can't come inside. Will you look after Toby for me?

Mrs Alexander   I really don't think that would be a good idea Christopher.

Where's your father at the moment Christopher?

Christopher   I don't know.

Mrs Alexander   Well perhaps we should try and give him a ring and see if we can get in touch with him. I'm sure he's worried about you. And I'm sure that there's been a dreadful misunderstanding.

Christopher *leaves.*

He goes back to his house.

He sees **Ed**'s *cashpoint card on the floor. He stares at it, frozen in his tracks.*

He approaches the card.

He takes it, puts it in his pocket.

Company   3558. 3558. 3558. 3558. 3558.

Christopher   3558.

He leaves the house.

*The **Company** make Swindon town centre.*

Christopher   Where can I buy a map?

Lady in Street   Pardon?

Christopher   Where can I buy a map?

Lady in Street   A map of where?

Christopher   A map of here.

Lady in Street   I don't know where do you want to get to?

Christopher   I'm going to the train station.

Lady in Street   You don't need a map to get to the train station.

Christopher   I do because I don't know where the train station is.

Lady in Street   You can see it from here.

Christopher   No I can't. And also I need to know where there is a cash machine.

Lady in Street   There. That building. Says signal point on the top. There's a British Rail sign on the other end. The station's at the bottom of that.

Christopher   Do you mean the stripey building with the horizontal windows that you can see poking out over those houses?

Lady in Street   That's the one.

Christopher   How do I get to that building?

Lady in Street   Gordon Bennett.

Christopher   I knew that the train station was somewhere near. And if something is nearby you can find it by moving in a spiral, walking clockwise and taking every right turn until you come back to a road you've already walked on, then taking the next left, then taking every right turn and so on.

And that was how I found the station.

The **Voices** *here are pre-recorded.*

Voice One   Customers seeking access to the car park please use assistance phone opposite, right of the ticket office

Voice Two   Warning CCTV in operation

Voice Three   Great Western

Voice Five   Cold beers and lagers

Voice Two   CAUTION WET FLOOR

Voice Four   Your 50p will keep a premature baby alive for 1.8 seconds

Voice Three   Transforming travel

Voice Five   Refreshingly Different

Voice One   It's delicious it's creamy and its only £1.30 Hot Choc Deluxe

Voice Two   0870 777 7676

Voice Four   The Lemon Tree

Voice One   No Smoking

Voice Two   Fine teas

Voice Five   Automatic Fire Door Keep Clear

Voice Two   Air Conditioned

Voice Three   Reserved Parking

Voice Four   Open As Usual This Way

Voice Three   No Smoking

Voice Five   No alcohol

Voice Three   Dogs must be carried

Voice One   RVP

Voice Three   Dogs must be carried

Voice One   LFB

Voice Four   A Perfect Blend

Voice Two   Royal Mail

Voice Four   Mon–Fri 7 am–7 pm

Voice Three   Dogs must be carried at all times

Voice Five   Special Lunch Offers

Voice One   Parking Subject to the Railway Byelaws Section 219 of the Transport Act 2000

Voice Three   Please stand on the right

Voice Four   Superb Coffee

Voice Two   Step-free Access

Voice Five   Take Extra Care with Children

Voice Four   Superb Coffee

Voice Three   Cash Dispensers

Voice Four   Superb Coffee

Voice Three   Dogs must be carried at all times

Station Policeman   Are you all right, young man?

Christopher   You're too old.

Station Policeman   Are you all right, young man?

Christopher   You're too old to play a policeman.

Station Policeman   Are you all right, young man?

Christopher   No.

Station Policeman   You're looking a bit worse for wear. The lady at the cafe says that when she tried talking to you, you were in a complete trance. What's your name?

Christopher   Christopher Boone.

Station Policeman   Where do you live?

Christopher   36 Randolph Street.

Station Policeman   What are you doing here?

Christopher   I needed to sit down and be quiet and think.

Station Policeman   OK let's keep it simple. What are you doing at the railway station?

Christopher   I'm going to see Mother.

Station Policeman   Mother?

Christopher   Yes, Mother.

Station Policeman   When's your train?

Christopher   I don't know. She lives in London. I don't know when there's a train to London.

Station Policeman   So, you don't live with your mother?

Christopher   No. But I'm going to.

Station Policeman   So where does your mother live.

Christopher   In London.

Station Policeman   Yes, but where in London.

Christopher   451c Chapter Road, London NW2 5NG.

Station Policeman   Jesus. What is that?

Christopher   That's Toby, my pet rat.

Station Policeman   A pet rat?

Christopher   Yes, a pet rat. He's very clean and he hasn't got bubonic plague.

Station Policeman   Well, that's reassuring.

Christopher   Yes.

Station Policeman   Have you got a ticket?

Christopher   No.

Station Policeman   So how precisely were you going to get to London then?

Christopher   I have a cashpoint card.

Station Policeman   Is this your card?

Christopher   No it's Father's.

Station Policeman   Father's.

Christopher   Yes, Father's.

Station Policeman   OK.

Christopher   He told me the number. It's 3558.

Station Policeman   Shhhh. Why don't you and I take a stroll to the cash machine, eh?

Christopher   You mustn't touch me.

Station Policeman   Why would I want to touch you?

Christopher   I don't know.

Station Policeman   Well, neither do I.

Christopher   Because I got a caution for hitting a policeman but I didn't mean to hurt him and if I do it again I'll get into even bigger trouble.

Voice One   Please insert your card.

Station Policeman   You're serious aren't you?

Christopher   Yes.

Voice One   Enter your personal identification number.

Station Policeman   You lead the way.

Christopher   Where?

Station Policeman   Back by the ticket office.

Voice One   Please enter amount. Ten pounds. Twenty pounds. Fifty pounds. One hundred pounds.

Christopher   How much does it cost to get a ticket to London?

Station Policeman   About twenty quid.

Voice One   Please wait. Your transaction is being processed.

Christopher   Is that pounds?

Station Policeman   Christ alive. Yep. Its twenty pounds.

Voice One   Please take your card and wait for your cash.

Beat.

Station Policeman   Well I guess I shouldn't keep you chatting any longer.

Christopher   Where do I get a ticket for the train from?

Station Policeman   You are a prize specimen aren't you?

Christopher   Where do I get a ticket for the train from?

Station Policeman   In there. Now are you sure you know what you're doing?

Christopher   Yes. I'm going to London to live with my mother.

Station Policeman   Has your mother got a telephone number?

Christopher   Yes.

Station Policeman   And can you tell me what it is?

Christopher   Yes. Its 020 8887 8907.

Station Policeman   And you'll ring her if you get into any trouble OK?

Christopher   I want to go to London.

Man behind Counter   If you don't mind.

Christopher   I want to go to London.

Man behind Counter   Single or return?

Christopher   What does single or return mean?

Man behind Counter   Do you want to go one way or do you want to come back?

Christopher   I want to stay there when I get there.

Man behind Counter   For how long?

Christopher   Until I go to university.

Man behind Counter   Single then. That'll be £17.

Christopher   When is the train to London?

Man behind Counter   Platform 1, five minutes.

Christopher   Where is Platform 1?

Man behind Counter   Through the underpass and up the stairs. You'll see the signs.

Somebody bumps into **Christopher**. *He barks at them like a dog.*

Siobhan   Underpass means tunnel Christopher.

In your head imagine a big red line across the floor. It starts at your feet and goes through the tunnel. And walk along the line. And count the rhythm in your head because that helps doesn't it? Like when you're doing music or when you're doing drumming. Left, right, left, right, left, right, left, right

Christopher   Left, right, left, right, left, right, left, right, left, right, left, right.

Christopher   Is this the train to London?

Station Policeman   Christopher. Caught you just in time. We've got your father at the police station. He's looking for you.

Christopher   I know.

Station Policeman   So why are you going to London?

Christopher   Because I'm going to live with Mother.

Station Policeman   Well I think your father might have something to say about that.

Christopher *tries to run.* **Station Policeman** *grabs him.* **Christopher** *screams.* **Station Policeman** *lets go.*

Station Policeman   OK, let's not get over-excited here. I'm going to take you back to the police station and you and me and your dad can sit down and have a little chat about who's going where.

Christopher   Have you arrested Father?

Station Policeman   Arrested him? What for?

Christopher   He killed a dog. With a garden fork. The dog was called Wellington.

Station Policeman   Well, we can talk about that as well. Right now, young man, I think you've done enough adventuring for one day.

The **Station Policeman** *reaches out to touch him.* **Christopher** *screams.*

Station Policeman   Now listen, you little monkey. You can either do what I say, or I'm going to have to make . . .

The train begins to move.

Shitting fuck.

Christopher   Why are you swearing? Have we started? Has the train started?

Station Policeman   Don't move.

Rob? Yeah it's Nigel. I'm stuck here on the bloody train Yeah. Don't even . . . Look. It stops at Didcot Parkway. So if you can get someone to meet me with a car . . . Cheers. Tell his old man we've got him but it's going to take a while, OK? Great. Let's get ourselves a seat. Park yourself. You are a bloody handful you are. Jeez.

Christopher   I see everything. Most other people are lazy. They never look at everything. They do what is called glancing, which is the same word for bumping off something and carrying on in almost the same direction. And the information in their head is really simple. For example, if they are on a train looking out of a window at the countryside it might be

Voice One   1. I am sitting on a train looking out at a field that is full of grass.

Voice Two   2. There are some cows in the field.

Voice Three   3. It is sunny with a few clouds.

Voice Four   4. There are some flowers in the grass.

Voice Five   5. There is a village in the distance.

Voice One   6. There is a fence at the edge of the field and it has a gate in.

Christopher   And then they would stop noticing anything because they would be thinking something else like

Voice Two   'I really want a bag of quavers'

Christopher   or

Voice One   'I'm worried that I might have left the gas cooker on.'

Christopher   or

Voice Four   'I wonder if Julie has given birth yet.'

Christopher   But if I am sitting looking out of the window of a train onto the countryside I notice everything. Like . . .

As he talks he raps out a nervous rhythm with his hand.

1. There are nineteen cows in the field. Fifteen of which are black and white and four of which are brown and white

2. There is a village in the distance, which has 31 visible houses

3. There are ridges in the field

4. There is a plastic bag from Asda

5. There is Coca-Cola

6. There is the snail

The snail

There are cows

The cows are facing

The snail

There are nimbostratus clouds

There is a wind

There is a hedge

There is a Boeing 747 400

There is a white Reebok trainer

There is graffiti

'Jane plus Ian 4 ever'

Station Policeman   Oh Christ, you've wet yourself. For God's sake go to the bloody toilet, will you?

Christopher   But I'm on a train.

Station Policeman   They do have toilets on trains, you know.

Christopher   Where is the toilet on the train?

Station Policeman   Through those doors there. But I'll be keeping an eye on you, you understand?

Christopher   No.

Station Policeman   Just go to the bloody toilet.

Christopher *stands.*

He walks down the corridor of the train. Shaking and closing his eyes he pisses.

He tries to wash his hands but can't because there is no running water.

He spits on his hands to wash them. He rubs them dry with toilet paper.

Shaking he leaves the toilet.

He goes to the luggage rack.

He climbs onto the shelf.

He hides himself.

He starts listing prime numbers to himself.

As he continues to count the **Station Policeman** *notices he's gone. The counting continues under the following exchanges.*

Christopher   2 3 5 7 11 13 17 19 23 29 31 37 41 43 47 53 59 61 67 71 73 79 83 89 97 101 103 107 109 113 127 131 137 139 149 151 157 163 167 173 179 181 191 193 197 199 211 223 227 229 233 239 241 251 257 263 269 271 277 281

Station Policeman   Christopher? Christopher? Bloody hell.

He leaves. **Christopher** *stays where he is. Still counting.* **Woman on Train** *approaches him to take her bag.*

Woman on Train   You scared the living daylights out of me. I think someone's out there on the platform looking for you.

Christopher   I know.

Woman on Train   Well. It's your look-out.

She takes her bag. She leaves. **Christopher** *stays hidden behind the smaller pile of bags. Still counting. A* **Posh Woman** *approaches. She takes her bag.*

Posh Woman   You're touching my bag!

Christopher　Yes.

She leaves. **Christopher** *stays hidden behind the still smaller pile of bags. Still counting. Two drunk men approach to take their bags.*

Drunk One　Come and look at this, Barry. They've got like, a train elf.

Drunk Two　Well we have both been drinking.

Drunk One　We should nick him.

Drunk Two　He could be our elf mascot.

Drunk One　Come on, shift it you daft twat. We've got a match to get to.

A lady takes her bag, it is the wrong one. She realises.

Voice One　Bollocks.

Another lady runs to grab her bag, she is talking to someone on the platform.

Voice Five　I'm coming alright. Wait for me in the car park.

Both ladies take the correct bag and leave **Christopher** *alone. He stops counting. He lies still for a while.*

He looks around. For the first time he is alone on stage.

Christopher　I waited for nine more minutes but nobody else came past and the train was really quiet. And I didn't move again. So I realised that the train had stopped. And I knew that the last stop on the train was London.

I heard the sound of feet and it was a policeman.

The **Station Policeman** *enters and explores the back of the stage.*

Station Policeman　Excuse me have you seen a 15-year-old boy he's . . . /

Christopher　/ Not the one who was on the train before.

The **Station Policeman** *looks at* **Christopher**. *Exits, disappointed. Is replaced by a* **London Transport Policeman**.

London Transport Policeman   Excuse me have you seen a 15-year-old boy he's wearing an orange jacket and a rucksack and he has a rat with him.

Christopher   And I could see him through the door, in the next carriage, and he was looking under the seats. I decided I didn't like policemen so much any more. So I got off the train.

He very tentatively gets down off the luggage rack and gets off the train.

Siobhan   Left, right, left, right, left, right . . .

Christopher   Left, right, left, right, left, right, left, right, left, right, left, right, left, right, left, right, left, right, left, right, left, right, left.

*These **Voices** are also pre-recorded*

Voice One   Sweet Pastries

Voice Two   Heathrow Airport Check In Here

Voice One   Bagel factory

Voice Five   EAT.

Voice Three   Excellence and taste

Voice Four   YO! Sushi

Voice One   Stationlink

Voice Two   Buses

Voice Five   WHSmith

Voice Four   Mezzanine

Voice One   Heathrow Express

Voice Two   Clinique

Voice Three   First Class Lounge

Voice Four   Fuller's

Voice Five   easyCar.com

Voice Two   The Mad Bishop

Voice Three   And Bear Public House

Voice Four   Fuller's London Pride

Voice One   Dixons

Voice Three   Paddington Bear at Paddington Station

Voice Five   Tickets

Voice One   Taxis

Voice Two   First Aid

Voice Four   Eastbourne Terrace

Voice Two   Way Out

Voice One   Praed Street

Voice Five   The Lawn

Voice Three   Q Here Please

Voice Four   Upper Crust

Voice One   Sainsbury's

Voice Five   Local information

Voice Three   Great Western First

Voice One   Position Closed

Voice Two   Closed

Voice Four   Position Closed

Voice Three   Sock Shop

Voice Four   Fast Ticket Point

Voice Five   Millie's Cookies

Voice One   Coffee

Voice Two   Fergie to Stay at Manchester United

Voice Three   Freshly Baked Cookies and Muffins

Voice Two   Cold Drinks

Voice Four   Penalty Fares

Voice One   Warning

Voice Three   Savoury Pastries

Voice Four   Platform 14

Voice Five   Burger King

Voice Two   Fresh Filled

Voice Three   The Reef Café Bar

Voice Four   Business travel

Voice One   Special Edition

Voice Two   Top 75 Albums

Voice Five   Evening Standard

As the chorus becomes more cacophonous **Christopher** *finds it more difficult to continue to walk.* **Christopher** *stops. Rests his head against a box. Puts his hands over his ears. A* **Station Guard** *approaches him.*

Station Guard   You look lost.

Christopher *pulls out his Swiss Army knife.*

The **Station Guard** *backs away.*

Station Guard   Whoa, whoa, whoa, whoa.

Christopher *carries on.*

Christopher   Left, right, left, right, left, right, left, right.

He makes his hand into a telescope to limit his field of vision.

He approaches an information counter.

Is this London?

Is this London?

Information   Sure is honey.

Christopher   Is this London?

Information   Indeed it is.

Christopher   How do I get to 451c Chapter Road, London NW2 5NG?

Information   Where is that?

Christopher   It's 451c Chapter Road, London, NW2 5NG. And sometimes you can write it 451c Chapter Road, Willesden, London, NW2 5NG.

Information   Take the Tube to Willesden Junction. Or Willesden Green. Got to be near there somewhere.

Christopher   What is a Tube?

Information   Are you for real? Over there. See that big staircase with the escalators? See the sign? Says Underground. Take the Bakerloo Line to Willesden Junction or the Jubilee to Willesden Green. You OK honey?

Ed   Don't do this Christopher.

Christopher   Get away from me.

Ed   Christopher, you won't be able to.

Christopher   I'm doing really well.

Ed   Where's your red line gone? See? It's disappeared hasn't it?

Where's your Swiss Army knife? Have you lost it?

Christopher   It's in my pocket.

Ed   Where?

Christopher   Here.

Ed   How the hell are you going to find the Jubilee Line. You don't even know what an escalator is, do you?

Christopher   It's a moving staircase. You step onto it. It carries you down. It's funny. Look.

Ed   Stop laughing. Everybody's looking at you.

Christopher   It's like something out of science fiction.

Ed   I'm worried about you.

Christopher   You're lying. You killed Wellington.

Ed   Where are you going?

Christopher   To watch the people. It's easy look. You go to the black machine. You look at where you want to go. You find the price. You put your money in.

Ed   You haven't got any money.

Christopher   I have. I stole your card.

Ed   You little shit.

Christopher   You press ticket type. You press adult single. £4.50. You insert £4.50. You take ticket and change. You go up to the grey gate. You put your ticket in the slot. It comes out of the other side.

Ed   There's no Jubilee Line. How are you going to get on the Jubilee Line to Willesden Green? You're in the wrong place.

Christopher   There's a Bakerloo Line. Look. I can go to Willesden Junction.

Ed   Come back home.

Christopher   I can't.

Ed   You can.

Christopher   You told a lie. You killed Wellington. Swindon's not my home anymore. My home is 451c Chapter Road, London NW2 5NG.

The Tube line appears.

Ed   Stand behind the yellow line.

Christopher   I know.

Ed   The train will be very noisy.

Christopher   I know.

Ed   It'll really scare you.

Christopher   I know.

Ed   Try not to let it. Watch what the people do. Watch how they get on and off.

Christopher   Yes.

The **Company** *stand with* **Christopher** *on the platform.*

Ed   Count the trains. Figure it out. Get the rhythm right.

Train coming. Train stopped. Doors open. Train going. Silence.

Train coming. Train stopped. Doors open. Train going. Silence.

Christopher   Train coming. Train stopped. Doors open. Train going. Silence.

Train coming. Train stopped. Doors open. Train going. Silence.

Train coming. Train stopped. Doors open. Train going. Silence.

Train coming. Train stopped. Doors open. Train going. Silence.

Train coming. Train stopped. Doors open . . .

He looks in **Toby**'*s cage. He can't find* **Toby**.

Christopher   Toby?

Toby?

Where are you?

Toby, Toby, what are you doing down there? Toby get back up here this instant. I'm warning you.

If you don't get back up here this instant then I will come down there to get you. Right. I'm coming down there Toby and when I catch you, I'm going to be very cross. I'm not going to let you play on your wheel for a whole week.

Man with Socks   Jesus what are you doing?

Christopher   My rat is on here.

Man with Socks   Get out of there for fuck's sake.

Christopher   Toby, it's filthy down here. You'll get so dirty.

Punk Girl   Oh my dayz. What is he doing?

Man with Socks   What does it sodding well look like he's doing?

Punk Girl   Call somebody. Get somebody. Don't just stand there.

Man with Socks   There's nobody to call. Mate please for Christ's sake please get back up here.

Christopher   I can't get back up there I need to get my rat.

Punk Girl   What?

Man with Socks   Mate, please, you're going to get yourself killed.

Punk Girl   You're going to have to go down there and get him.

Man with Socks   Me? What the hell has it got to do with me?

Punk Girl   He's a kid. You can't just let him get hit.

Man with Socks   Yes I know he's a kid. I can see he's a kid by sodding well looking at him. Mate. Please come on.

Christopher   You're so silly. What am I going to do with you Toby?

Stop being so difficult.

Man with Socks   I don't believe this is happening. This is ridiculous, mate get your arse out of there now.

Tube train starts rumbling

Christopher   Don't panic, I found him.

Punk Girl   Help him den, you muppet.

Man with Socks   Oh Christ. Oh Christ.

Christopher *and* **Toby** *are back on the platform.*

Man with Socks   What the fuck do you think you were playing at?

Christopher   I was finding Toby. He's my pet rat.

Man with Socks   Fucking Nora.

Punk Girl   Is he OK?

Man with Socks   Him? Thanks a fucking bundle. Jesus Christ. A pet rat. Oh shit. My train. Fuck.

He leaves.

Punk Girl   Are you OK?

She touches **Christopher**'*s arm. He screams.*

Punk Girl   OK. OK. OK. Is there anything I can do to help you?

Christopher   Stand further away. I've got a Swiss Army knife and it has a saw blade and it could cut someone's finger off.

Punk Girl   OK buddy. I'm going to take that as a no.

She leaves. **Christopher** *counts the trains again.*

Christopher   Train coming. Train stopped. Doors open. Train going.

He groans.

Train coming. Train stopped. Doors open. Train going.

He groans.

Train coming. Train stopped. Doors open.

He is bundled onto the train.

Christopher   Is this train going to Willesden Junction?

The **Voices** *here are pre-recorded*

Voice One   There are 53,963 holiday cottages in Scandinavia and Germany.

Voice Two   VITABIOTICS

Christopher   Is this train going to Willesden Junction?

Voice Three   3435

Voice Five   Penalty £10 if you fail to show a valid ticket for your entire journey

Voice Four   Discover Gold, Then Bronze

Christopher   Is this train going to Willesden Junction?

Voice One   TVIC

Voice Three   EPBIC

Voice Two   Suck my cock

Voice Five   Obstructing the doors can be dangerous

Voice Two   BRV

Voice Three   Con. IC

Christopher   Is this train going to Willesden Junction?

Voice Four   TALK TO THE WORLD

Voice One   Warwick Avenue

Maida Vale

Kilburn Park

Queen's Park

Kensal Green

Willesden Junction

Christopher   Where is 451c Chapter Road, London NW2 5NG?

*A **Shopkeeper** shows him an A–Z of London.*

Shopkeeper   A to Z of London. Two ninety-five. Are you going to buy it or not?

Christopher   I don't know.

Shopkeeper   Well you can get your dirty fingers off it if you don't mind.

Christopher   Where is 451c Chapter Road, London NW2 5NG?

Shopkeeper   You can either buy the A to Z or you can hop it. I'm not a walking encyclopaedia.

Christopher   Is that the A to Z?

Shopkeeper   No, it's a sodding crocodile.

Christopher   Is that the A to Z?

Shopkeeper   Yes it's the A to Z.

Christopher   Can I buy it?

Shopkeeper   Two pounds ninety-five, but you're giving me the money first. I'm not having you scarpering.

Christopher *examines the A–Z. He opens it. He looks for Chapter Road.*

Man on Phone *approaches him.*

Man on Phone   Big cheese. Oh yes. The nurses. Never. Bloody liar. Total. Bloody liar.

He leaves.

Christopher *closes the map. His voice quietens the more he talks. And as he talks he squats. And then huddles into a ball.*

Christopher   Left. Right. Left. Right. Left. Right.

Left.

Right.

Left.

Right.

Left.

Right.

Left.

He sits silently, huddled for a while.

Judy *and* **Roger** *enter.*

Judy   I don't care whether you thought it was funny or not.

Roger   Judy look, I'm sorry OK.

Judy   Well perhaps you should have thought about that before you made me look like a complete idiot.

Christopher *stands up.* **Judy** *sees him.*

The two look at one another.

Christopher   You weren't in so I waited for you.

Judy   Christopher.

Christopher   What?

Judy   Christopher.

She goes to hug him. He pushes her away so hard that he falls over.

Roger   What the hell is going on?

Judy   I'm so sorry Christopher. I forgot.

Judy *spreads her fingers.* **Christopher** *spreads his to touch hands with her.*

Roger   I suppose this means Ed's here.

Judy   Where's your father Christopher?

Christopher   I think he's in Swindon.

Roger   Thank God for that.

Judy   But how did you get here?

Christopher   I came on the train.

Judy   Oh my God Christopher. I didn't . . . I didn't think I'd ever . . . Why are you here on your own?

Christopher, you're soaking. Roger, don't just stand there.

Roger   Are you going to come in or are you going to stand out here all night?

Christopher   I'm going to live with you because Father killed Wellington with a garden fork.

Roger   Jumping Jack Christ.

Judy   Roger, please. Come on Christopher. Let's go inside and get you dried off.

Roger   Come on then Soldier, let's get you warmed up. You'll catch your death out here.

Christopher *doesn't move.*

Judy   You follow Roger.

Christopher *doesn't move. He gives* **Toby** *to* **Roger**.

Christopher   He's hungry. Have you got any food I can give him and some water?

Judy   Are you OK Christopher?

Christopher   I'm very tired.

Judy   I know love. Will you let me help you get your clothes off. I can get you a clean T-shirt. You could get yourself into bed.

She leaves the bedroom and gets **Roger** *to pass her a T-shirt.*

Judy   T-shirt, pass me a T-shirt.

She goes back into **Christopher**'s *room and changes him. He wears one of her old T-shirts.*

Judy   You're very brave.

Christopher   Yes.

Judy   You never wrote to me.

Christopher   I know.

Judy   Why didn't you write to me, Christopher? I wrote you all those letters. I kept thinking something dreadful had happened or you'd moved away and I'd never find out where you were.

Christopher   Father said you were dead.

Judy   What?

Christopher   He said you went into hospital because you had something wrong with your heart. And then you had a heart attack and died.

Judy   Oh my God.

She starts to howl.

Christopher   Why are you doing that?

Judy   Oh Christopher, I'm so sorry.

Christopher   It's not your fault.

Judy   Bastard. The Bastard.

Christopher, let me hold your hand. Just for once. Just for me. Will you? I won't hold it hard.

Christopher   I don't like people holding my hand.

Judy   No. OK. That's OK.

London Policeman   I need to speak to him.

Judy   He's been through enough today already.

London Policeman   I know. But I still need to speak to him.

Christopher Boone. Please can you open the door.

Roger   Come on Christopher.

Judy   Christopher love. It's all right. Just open the door will you sweetheart?

Christopher   Is he going to take me away?

Judy   No Christopher he isn't.

Christopher   Will you let him take me away?

Judy   No. I won't.

Christopher   Do you promise?

Judy   Yes. I promise.

London Policeman   Your father says you've run away. Is that right?

Christopher   Yes.

London Policeman   Is this your mother?

Christopher Yes.

London Policeman Why did you run away?

Christopher Because Father killed Wellington who is a dog and so that meant that he could kill me.

London Policeman So I've been told. Do you want to go back to Swindon to your father or do you want to stay here?

Christopher I want to stay here.

London Policeman And how do you feel about that?

Christopher I want to stay here.

London Policeman Hang on, I'm asking your mother.

Judy He told Christopher I was dead.

London Policeman OK. Let's . . . let's not get into an argument about who said what here. I just want to know whether . . .

Judy Of course he can stay.

London Policeman Well I think that probably settles it as far as I'm concerned.

Christopher Are you going to take me back to Swindon?

London Policeman No.

If your husband turns up and causes any trouble, just give us a ring. Otherwise you're going to have to sort this out among yourselves.

Ed I'm talking to her whether you like it or not.

Judy Roger. Don't. Just . . .

Roger I'm not going to be spoken to like that in my own home.

Ed I'll talk to you how I damn well like.

Judy   You have no right to be here.

Ed   He's my son in case you've forgotten.

Judy   What in God's name did you think you were playing at saying those things to him?

Ed   You were the one that bloody left.

Judy   So, you decided to just wipe me out of his life altogether?

Roger   Now let's just all calm down here, shall we?

Ed   Well, isn't that what you wanted?

Judy   I wrote to him every week.

Ed   What the fuck use is writing to him?

Roger   Whoa. Whoa. Whoa.

Ed   I cooked his meals. I cleaned his clothes. I looked after him every weekend; I looked after him when he was ill. I took him to the doctor. I worried myself sick every time he wandered off somewhere at night. I went to school every time he got into a fight. And you? What? You wrote him some fucking letters.

Christopher *gets up out of the sleeping bag.*

Judy   So you thought it was OK to tell him his mother was dead?

Roger   Now is not the time.

Christopher *finds his Swiss Army knife.*

Ed   I'm going to see him. And if you try to stop me . . .

He gets into **Christopher**'s *room.* **Christopher** *points his knife at him.*

Judy *comes in.*

Judy   It's OK Christopher I won't let him do anything. You're all right.

Ed   Christopher?

Ed *squats down, completely exhausted.*

Christopher *still points the knife at him.*

Ed   Christopher I'm really, really sorry. About –. About –. About the letters. I never meant . . . I promise I will never do anything like that again.

Ed *spreads his fingers and tries to get* **Christopher** *to touch him.* **Christopher** *ignores him. He still holds his knife out. He groans.*

Ed   Shit. Christopher, please.

London Policeman   Mr Boone.

Ed   What the fuck are you doing here? Did you call him?

London Policeman   Mr Boone, come on mate.

Ed   Don't fucking mate me. This is my son.

London Policeman   I know. This can all be sorted out. Just come with me. Please.

Judy   I think you should go now. I think he's frightened.

Ed   I'll be back.

Christopher. I'll be back. I promise you Christopher. I promise you lad.

Christopher *groans.*

London Policeman *makes* **Ed** *leave.*

Roger *watches them both leave.*

Judy *and* **Christopher** *are left alone together.*

Judy   You go back to sleep now. Everything is going to be all right. I promise.

They leave **Christopher** *in his room. He lies down. He settles.*

Immediately **Christopher** *has settled it is the next morning.* **Roger** *and* **Judy** *give him breakfast. He is overwhelmed by them.*

Roger   OK. He can stay for a few days.

Judy   He can stay as long as he needs to stay.

Roger   This flat is hardly big enough for two people, let alone three.

Judy   He can understand what you're saying, you know?

Roger   What's he going to do? There's no school for him to go to. We've both got jobs. It's bloody ridiculous.

He gives **Christopher** *a strawberry milkshake.*

Judy   Roger. That's enough. You can stay as long as you want to stay.

Christopher   It was Mother who gave me the milkshake.

They look at him.

It was Mother who gave me the milkshake not you.

Judy *picks the milkshake up.*

Christopher   You need to shout more loudly at him. Like you're really angry with him not just being nice.

Judy *looks at him. Nods.*

Judy   OK.

She puts the milkshake down. She's much angrier.

Roger. That's enough. You can stay as long as you want to stay.

She looks at **Christopher** *examining his response. Expecting more feedback.*

Christopher   I have to go back to Swindon.

They both look at him.

Judy   Christopher you've only just got here.

Christopher   I have to go back because I have to sit my Maths A level.

Judy   You're doing Maths A level?

Christopher   Yes. I'm taking it on Wednesday and Thursday and Friday next week.

Judy   God.

Christopher   The Reverend Peters is going to be the invigilator.

Judy   I mean that's really good.

Christopher   I'm going to get an A* grade. And that's why I have to go back to Swindon. Except I can't see Father. So I have to go back to Swindon with you.

Judy   I don't know whether that's going to be possible.

Christopher   But I have to go.

Judy   Let's talk about this some other time, OK?

Christopher   OK. But I have to go to Swindon.

He stands and leaves.

Judy   Christopher. Please.

Christopher   What time is it?

Siobhan   Seven minutes past two in the morning.

Christopher   I can't sleep.

Siobhan   It's because you're scared of Mr Shears. You're being silly.

Christopher   There's nobody about. You can hear traffic.

He wanders down the street.

Siobhan   What cars are there?

Christopher   A Fiesta. A Nissan Micra. A Peugeot. A Ford Granada.

Siobhan   What colours are they?

Christopher   I can't tell. I can only see orange and black. And mixtures of orange and black.

Siobhan   Look at the things people have in their front garden.

Christopher   Oh yes. Is that an elf?

Siobhan   It's a gnome. And a teddy bear. And a little pond look.

Christopher   And a cooker.

I like looking up at the sky.

Siobhan   Me too.

Christopher   When you look at the sky at night you know you are looking at stars, which are hundreds and thousands of light years away from you. And some of the stars don't exist any more because their light has taken so long to get to us that they are already dead, or they have exploded and collapsed into red dwarfs. And that makes you seem very small, and if you have difficult things in your life it is nice to think that they are what is called negligible which means they are so small you don't have to take them into account when you are calculating something. I can't see any stars here.

Siobhan   No.

Christopher   It's because of all the light pollution in London. All the light from the streetlights and car headlights and floodlights and lights in the buildings reflect off tiny particles in the atmosphere and they get in the way of light from the stars.

Judy   Christopher?

She starts looking for **Christopher**.

Siobhan   I have to go.

Christopher   Don't.

Siobhan   I have to.

Christopher   Siobhan? Siobhan? Where are you going? Siobhan?

Judy   Christopher? Christopher?

Christopher *stands up*. **Judy** *stares at him*.

Judy   Jesus Christ. What are you doing out here? I've been looking for you. I thought you'd gone. If you ever do that again, I swear to God, Christopher, I love you, but . . . I don't know what I'll do.

You need to promise me you won't leave the flat on your own again Christopher. Christopher do you promise me that?

Christopher   Yes.

Judy   You can't trust people in London.

Roger   Don't be a bloody fool.

Judy   I'm not being a bloody fool, Roger, they got somebody in. They didn't even call me. They didn't ask me if I wanted to come back. I've been off two days. It's illegal that is.

Roger   It was a temporary job, for Christ's sake.

Christopher   I have to go to Swindon to take my A level.

Judy   Christopher, not now.

I'm getting phone calls from your father threatening to take me to court. I'm getting it in the neck from Roger. It's not a good time.

Christopher   But I have to go because it's been arranged and the Reverend Peters is going to invigilate.

Judy   It's only an exam. I can ring the school. We can get it postponed. You can take it some other time.

Christopher   I can't take it another time. It's been arranged. And I've done lots of revision. And Mrs Gascoyne says we could use a room at school.

Judy   Christopher I am just about holding this together. But I am this close to losing it, all right? So just give me some . . .

She breaks. She cries. She holds her fist to her mouth to try to stop herself.

She leaves the room. She comes back.

Judy   Would you like an iced lolly?

Christopher   Yes I would please.

Judy   Would you like a strawberry one?

Christopher   Yes I would please because that's red. What's it called here?

Judy   It's called Hampstead Heath. I love it. You can see all over London.

Christopher   Where are the planes going to?

Judy   Heathrow I think.

Christopher I rang Mrs Gascoyne.

I told her that you're going to take your Maths A level next year.

Christopher *screams. He throws his iced lolly away.*

Judy   Christopher please. Calm down. OK. OK Christopher. Just calm down love.

Woman on Heath   Is he OK?

Judy   Well, what does it look like to you?

Christopher *screams and screams. He only stops because his chest hurts and he runs out of breath.*

Roger *gives* **Christopher** *a radio and three children's books.*

Roger   Here we are. You wanted a radio. *100 Number Puzzles*. It's from the library. This one is called *The Origins of the Universe*. And this one is *Nuclear Power*.

Christopher   They're for children.

They're not very good.

I'm not going to read them.

Roger   Well, it's nice to know my contribution is appreciated.

Judy   Christopher I made you a chart. Because you've got to eat love. In here is some Complan and it's got strawberry flavouring in it.

Roger   Complan?

Judy   Be quiet Roger. Christopher if you drink 200ml then I'm going to put a bronze star on your chart.

Roger   I don't believe this.

Judy   Roger for God's sake, please. If you drink 400ml you get a silver star.

Roger   Ha!

Judy   And if you drink 600ml you get a gold star.

Roger   A gold star. Well that's very original I have to say.

Judy   Roger stop it. You're not helping.

Christopher *picks up the radio. He leaves. He de-tunes it so that it is between two stations. He listens to the white noise. He turns the volume up very high.*

Some time.

Roger *watches him. He opens and drinks four cans of lager. He necks the lager in one go.*

Roger *comes into* **Christopher**'s *room. He is very drunk.*

Roger   You think you're so clever, don't you? Don't you ever, ever think about other people for one second, eh? Well I bet you're really pleased with yourself now aren't you?

He grabs at **Christopher**. **Christopher** *rolls himself into a ball to hide.*

Judy *comes into the room. She grabs* **Roger**. *She pulls him away from* **Christopher**.

Christopher *is moaning still in his ball.*

Judy   Christopher, I'm sorry. I'm really, really sorry. I promise this will never happen again.

He remains in his ball.

He doesn't stop moaning.

Judy *and* **Roger** *leave.*

Eventually he calms.

Christopher   What time is it?

Judy   It's four o'clock.

Christopher   What are you doing?

Judy   I'm packing some clothes.

Christopher   Where's Mr Shears?

Judy   He is asleep.

Come downstairs. Bring Toby. Get into the car.

Christopher   Into Mr Shears' car?

Judy   That's right.

Christopher   Are you stealing the car?

Judy   I'm just borrowing it.

Christopher   Where are we going?

Judy   We're going home.

Christopher   Do you mean home in Swindon?

Judy   Yes.

Christopher   Is Father going to be there?

Judy   Please, Christopher. Don't give me any hassle right now, OK?

Christopher   I don't want to be with Father.

Judy   Just . . . just . . . it's going to be all right, Christopher, OK? It's going to be all right?

Christopher   Are we going back to Swindon so I can do my Maths A Level?

Judy   What?

Christopher   I'm meant to be doing my Maths A level tomorrow.

Judy   We're going back to Swindon because if we stay in London any longer . . . someone was going to get hurt. And I don't necessarily mean you.

Now I need you to be quiet for a while.

Christopher   How long do you need me to be quiet for?

Judy   Jesus. Half an hour Christopher. I need you to be quiet for half an hour.

Ed   How the fuck did you get in here?

Judy   This is my house too, in case you've forgotten?

Ed   Is your fancy man here, as well?

Christopher *starts drumming on one of the boxes. He begins drumming on them. He drums and drums and drums.* **Ed** *and* **Judy** *talking inaudibly under the drumming.*

Judy   Christopher. Christopher.

He's gone. You don't need to panic.

Christopher   Where's he gone to?

Judy   He's gone to stay with Rhodri for a while.

Christopher   Is he going to be arrested? And go to prison?

Judy   What for?

Christopher   For killing Wellington.

Judy   I don't think so. I think he'll only get arrested if Mrs Shears presses charges.

Christopher   What's that?

Judy   It's when you tell the police to arrest somebody for little crimes. They only arrest people for little crimes if you ask them.

Christopher   Is killing Wellington a little crime?

Judy   Yes love it is.

In the next few weeks we're going to try and get a place of our own to live in.

Christopher   Can I do my Maths A level?

Judy   You're not listening to me are you, Christopher?

Christopher   I am listening to you.

Judy   I told you. I rang your headmistress. I told her you were in London. I told her you'd do it next year.

Christopher   But I'm here now so I can take it.

Judy   I'm sorry Christopher. I didn't know we'd be coming back. This isn't going to solve anything.

Mrs Shears   You've got a nerve.

Christopher   Where are we going?

Mrs Shears   Swanning round here as though nothing ever happened.

Judy   Ignore her Christopher.

Mrs Shears   So he's finally dumped you too has he?

Christopher   Where are we going?

Mrs Shears   You had it coming. Don't try and pretend that you didn't. Because you did.

Christopher   Where are we going?

Judy   We're going to the school.

Siobhan   So you're Christopher's mother.

Judy   That's right. And you're . . .

Siobhan   I'm Siobhan. It's nice to meet you.

Judy   Yeah. Yes. Yes. It's nice to meet you too.

Siobhan   Hello Christopher.

Christopher   Hello.

Siobhan   Are you OK?

Christopher   I'm tired.

Judy   He's a bit upset.

Siobhan   Because of the A level, you said.

Judy   He won't eat. He won't sleep.

Siobhan   Yeah.

I spoke to Mrs Gascoyne after you called.

Judy   Right.

Siobhan   She still actually has your A level papers in the three sealed envelopes in her desk.

Mrs Gascoyne   I still actually have the A level papers in my desk.

Christopher   Does that mean I can still do my A level?

Siobhan   I think so. We're going to ring the Reverend Peters to make sure he can still come in this afternoon and be your invigilator. And Mrs Gascoyne is going to call the examination board to say that you're going to take the exam after all. I thought I should tell you now. So you could think about it.

Christopher   So I could think about what?

Siobhan   Is this what you want to do Christopher? If you say you don't want to do it no one is going to be angry with you. And it won't be wrong or illegal or stupid. It will just be what you want and that will be fine.

Christopher   I want to do it.

Siobhan   OK.

How tired are you?

Christopher   Very.

Siobhan   How's your brain when you think about Maths?

Christopher   I don't think it really works very well.

Siobhan   What's the logarithmic formula for the approximate number of prime numbers not greater than x?

Christopher   I can't think.

Reverend Peters *enters. He picks up one envelope. He opens it. He looks at it. He carefully places it face down on* **Christopher***'s table.*

He goes to sit opposite him. He takes out a stopwatch.

Reverend Peters So this is jolly exciting, eh Christopher? Well I'm excited anyway. Now the exam is going to last for 90 minutes Christopher, OK? First thing to do is to pop your name on the front. OK young man, are you ready to roll? Turn over the paper please Christopher. And begin.

Christopher *turns over the exam paper.*

He stares at it.

He can't understand any questions. He panics. His breathing becomes erratic. To calm himself he counts the cubes of cardinal numbers.

Christopher 1, 8, 27, 64, 125, 216, 343, 512, 729, 1000, 1331.

Reverend Peters Are you all right Christopher?

Christopher I can't read the question.

Reverend Peters What do you mean?

Christopher I can't read the question.

Reverend Peters Can you see the question?

Christopher I can see the questions but I can't read the questions because when I look at the words they all seem confused and the wrong way round and mixed up to me.

Reverend Peters Right.

Christopher What does this question say?

Reverend Peters Christopher I'm afraid I can't help you like that. I'm not allowed to.

Christopher *groans.*

Siobhan Christopher. Stop groaning. Get your breath. Count the cubes of the cardinal numbers again.

Christopher   1, 8, 27, 64, 125, 216, 343, 512, 729, 1000, 1331.

Siobhan   Now. Have another go.

He looks at the questions again.

Christopher   Show that a triangle with sides that can be written in the form n squared plus one, n squared minus one and two n (where n is greater than one) is right angled.

Siobhan   You don't have to tell us.

Christopher   What?

Siobhan   You don't have to tell us how you solved it.

Christopher   But it's my favourite question.

Siobhan   Yes but it's not very interesting.

Christopher   I think it is.

Siobhan   Christopher people won't want to hear about the answer to a maths question in a play.

Look why don't you tell it after the curtain call?

When you've finished you can do a bow and then people who want to can go home and if anybody wants to find out how you solved the maths question then they can stay and you can tell them at the end.

OK?

Christopher   OK.

He picks up his pencil.

He starts answering.

Ed *enters.*

Judy *is behind him.*

Ed   Don't scream.

OK, Christopher. I'm not going to hurt you.

He crouches down by **Christopher**.

Ed   I wanted to ask you how the exam went.

Judy   Tell him Christopher.

Please Christopher.

Christopher   I don't know if I got all the questions right because I was really tired and I hadn't eaten any food so I couldn't think properly.

Ed *nods. There is some time.*

Ed   Thank you.

Christopher   What for?

Ed   Just . . . thank you. I'm very proud of you Christopher. Very proud. I'm sure you did really well.

Siobhan   How's your flat?

Christopher   It's not really a flat. It's a room. It's small. The corridor's painted brown. Other people use the toilet. Mother has to clean the toilet before I can use it. Sometimes there are other people in there so I do wet myself. The corridor smells like gravy and bleach. The room smells like socks and pine air freshener. And another bad thing is that Toby died. Because he was two years and seven months old which is very old for a rat. I don't like waiting for my A level result.

If I was living at your house I would have room to put all my things and I wouldn't have to share the toilet with strangers.

Can I come and live in your house so that I'll have room to put all my things and I won't have to share the toilet with strangers?

Siobhan   No, Christopher. You can't.

Christopher   Why can't I? Is it because I'm too noisy and sometimes I'm 'difficult to control'.

Siobhan   No. It's because I'm not your mother Christopher.

Christopher   No.

Siobhan   That's very important, Christopher. Do you understand that?

Christopher   I don't know.

Mother doesn't get back from work till 5.30. So I have to go to Father's house between 3.49 and 5.30 because I'm not allowed to be on my own. Mother said I didn't have a choice. I pushed the bed up against the door in case Father tries to come in. Sometimes he tries to talk to me through the door. I don't answer him. Sometimes he sits outside the door quietly for a long time.

Ed enters. He's holding a kitchen timer.

Ed   Christopher, can I have a talk with you?

Christopher turns away from **Siobhan**.

Christopher   No. No. No. No. No. No you can't. No.

Judy   It's OK. I'll be here.

Christopher   I don't want to talk to Father.

Ed   I'll do you a deal. Five minutes OK? That's all.

He sets the timer for five minutes. It starts ticking.

Christopher, look . . . Things can't go on like this. I don't know about you, but this . . . this just hurts too much. You being in the house but refusing to talk to me. You have to learn to trust me . . . And I don't care how long it takes . . . if it's a minute one day and two minutes the next and three minutes the next and it takes years I don't care. Because this is important. This is more important than anything else.

Let's call it . . . let's call it a project. A project we have to do
together. You have to spend more time with me. And I . . . I
have to show you that you can trust me. And it will be
difficult at first because . . . because it's a difficult project. But
it will get better I promise. You don't have to say anything,
not right now. You have to think about it. And, . . . I've got
you a present. To show you that I really mean what I say.
And to say sorry. And because . . . well you'll see what I
mean.

He leaves.

*He comes back with a big cardboard box. It is importantly cardboard
and different to the other boxes. There's a blanket in it. He puts his
hands in the box. He takes out a little sandy coloured Golden
Retriever.*

Ed   He's two months old.

Christopher   I would never ever do anything to hurt you.

The dog sits on **Christopher**'s *lap.*

Judy   You won't be able to take him away with you I'm
afraid. The bedsit's too small. But your father's going to look
after him here. And you can come and take him out for
walks whenever you want.

Christopher   Does he have a name?

Ed   No. You can decide what to call him.

Christopher   Sandy. He's called Sandy.

The alarm goes off.

They look at each other.

Judy   We need to go now.

Ed   Yes.

Judy   We'll come back tomorrow and you can see him then.

Siobhan   Christopher.

Christopher   Yes.

Siobhan   Here.

Christopher   What's this?

Siobhan   It's your result Christopher.

Christopher   Right.

Siobhan   You need to open it and read it.

Christopher   Right.

He does.

Siobhan   Well? What does it say?

Christopher   I got an A*.

Siobhan   Oh. Oh. That's just. That's terrific Christopher.

Christopher   Yes.

Siobhan   Aren't you happy?

Christopher   Yes. It's the best result.

Siobhan   I know it is. How's your dog?

Christopher   He's very well. I stayed last week at father's because Mother got flu and he slept on my bed so he can bark in case anybody comes into my room at night.

Siobhan   Right. How are you getting on with your father Christopher?

Christopher   He planted a vegetable patch in his garden. I helped him and Sandy watched. We planted carrots and peas and spinach and I'm going to pick them when they're ready. He bought me a book, which is called *Further Maths for A Level*. He told Mrs Gascoyne that I'm going to take Further Maths next year. She said OK.

Mrs Gascoyne   OK.

Siobhan   I heard that.

Christopher   I'm going to pass it and get an A* grade. And then in two years I'll take A level physics and get an A* grade. And then I'm going to go to university in another town. It doesn't have to be in London because I don't like London and there are universities in lots of places and not all of them are in big cities. I can live in a flat with a garden and a proper toilet. I can take Sandy and my books and my computer. Then I will get a First Class Honours Degree. Then I will be a scientist. I can do these things.

Siobhan   I hope so.

Christopher   I can because I went to London on my own.

She looks at him.

I solved the mystery of Who Killed Wellington.

She looks at him.

I found my mother. I was brave.

Siobhan   You were.

Christopher   And I wrote a book.

Siobhan   I know. I read it. We turned it into a play.

Christopher   Yes. Does that mean I can do anything do you think?

Does that mean I can do anything Siobhan?

Does that mean I can do anything?

The two look at each other for a while.

Lights black.

After the curtain call **Christopher** *returns to the stage. He gets the attention of anybody still in the audience. Even if it is just one person. He thanks them for staying.*

Using as much theatricality as we can throw at it, using music, lights, sound, lasers, the boxes, the train tracks, the rest of the company, the orchestra, the fucking ushers for Christ's sake, using dance, song, bells, whistles, the works, he proves by means of a counter-example that when a triangle with sides that can be written in the form n squared plus one, n squared minus one and two n (where n is greater than one) is right angled.

Maths Appendix

After the applause, lights down, smoke, **Christopher** *appears rising through the centre trap. There is very cool, electro music.*

Thank you very much for clapping and thank you very much for staying behind to listen to how I answered the question on my maths A level. Siobhan said it wouldn't be very interesting but I said it was.

She didn't tell me what I should use, so I decided to use all the machines and computers in the theatre including: VL000 arc lights, which are moving lights, light emitting diodes, JBL control speakers, a Countryman boom mic and radio transmitter, 4 PTDX Panasonic overhead projectors and our DSM called Cynthia who will operate these.

I had ninety minutes to answer ten questions – but I spent thirty minutes doing groaning which meant I only had six minutes to answer this question.

A timer is projected – displaying 6.00.00.

Show that, a triangle with sides that can be written in the form n squared plus one, n squared minus one and two n (where n is greater than one) is right angled.

And this is what I wrote.

He runs and starts the timer.

Start the clock.

A right-angled triangle is made using projection (or lasers if you have the money, or holograms if you are in the future).

If a triangle is right angled, one of its angles will be 90 degrees and will therefore follow Pythagoras' theorem.

Pythagoras said that a squared plus b squared equals c squared.

To put it simply, if you draw squares outside the three sides of a right-angled triangle then add up the area of the two smaller squares, this will be equal to the area of the larger square. This is only true if the triangle is right angled.

Come on Bluey!

The A level question is an algebraic formula for making right-angled triangles. Algebra is like a computer program that works for whatever numbers you put into it.

To find the area of a square you must multiply the length by the width.

So . . . the area of this square is $2n \times 2n$.

Which equals 4n squared.

The area of this square is (n squared – 1) $\times$ (n squared – 1).

Which equals n to the power of four – 2n squared plus 1.

Then, if we add these two squares together . . .

This equals *n to the power of 4 plus 2n squared plus 1*.

NOW . . . We need to find the area of square on the hypotenuse which is (n to the power of $2 + 1$) x (n to the power of $2 + 1$).

Which equals *n to the power of 4 plus 2n squared plus 1*.

Which is THE SAME TERM!

So the area of the two small squares adds up to the area of the larger square. So all my squares fit together to satisfy Pythagoras' theorem. So the triangle is – RIGHT ANGLED!

Quod. Erat. Demonstrandum

And that is how I go an A*.

Confetti.

He exits.